The Complete Guide to

FINISHING BASEMENTS + GARAGES

Updated 3rd Edition

Projects and Practical Solutions for
Finishing Basements and Upgrading Garages

COOL
SPRINGS
PRESS

Quarto.com

© 2009–2024 Quarto Publishing Group USA Inc.

Second edition published in 2013; First edition 2009.

First Published in 2009 by Creative Publishing international, now Cool Springs Press, an imprint of The Quarto Group, 100 Cummings Center, Suite 265-D, Beverly, MA 01915, USA.

T (978) 282-9590 F (978) 283-2742

Cool Springs Press titles are also available at discount for retail, wholesale, promotional, and bulk purchase. For details, contact the Special Sales Manager by email at specialsales@quarto.com or by mail at The Quarto Group, Attn: Special Sales Manager, 100 Cummings Center, Suite 265-D, Beverly, MA 01915, USA.

28 27 26 25 24   1 2 3 4 5

ISBN: 978-0-7603-8888-4

Digital edition published in 2024

eISBN: 978-0-7603-8889-1

Page Layout: *tabula rasa* graphic design

Photography: See Photo Credits on page 237

New Illustrations: Ada Keesler on pages 80-83, 98-101, 108-109, 220-221; Christopher Mills on page 219

Printed in China

The Complete Guide to Finishing Basements + Garages

Created by: The Editors of Cool Springs Press, in cooperation with BLACK+DECKER.

BLACK+DECKER and the BLACK+DECKER logo are trademarks of The Black & Decker Corporation and are used under license. All rights reserved.

NOTICE TO READERS

For safety, use caution, care, and good judgment when following the procedures described in this book. The publisher and BLACK+DECKER cannot assume responsibility for any damage to property or injury to persons as a result of misuse of the information provided.

The techniques shown in this book are general techniques for various applications. In some instances, additional techniques not shown in this book may be required. Always follow manufacturers' instructions included with products, since deviating from the directions may void warranties. The projects in this book vary widely as to skill levels required: some may not be appropriate for all do-it-yourselfers, and some may require professional help.

Consult your local building department for information on building permits, codes, and other laws as they apply to your project.

Contents

The Complete Guide to Finishing Basements + Garages

Contents
(Cont.)

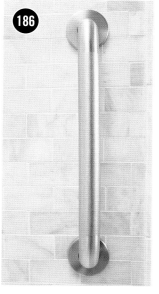

Introduction

An unfinished basement or garage can be a hidden treasure for any homeowner. Basements offer isolation for uses that might not be appropriate in the home's current floor plan, such as a small recording studio or party room. Garages provide accessible storage and are naturally adaptable to a number of functions.

The common criticisms of these spaces—that they are often dark and chilly—can be turned into assets. A light-starved room may be perfect for a showstopping home theater, while the natural insulation around a basement ensures a cool space in the summer and a warm one in the winter, without using much energy to heat or air condition the space.

This new edition of *Black + Decker Complete Guide to Basements + Garages* covers the many factors involved in turning a basement or garage into a dream space. As the new title shows, we've expanded this edition to cover garage conversions, because those structures are the aboveground equivalent of basements. Some houses don't have basements, but most do have garages. The considerations in converting either space are similar.

As the real estate market continues its decades-long upward trajectory, usable space becomes even more valuable. A simple basement or garage renovation can increase the home's value for a potential sale or improve the livability and enjoyment if moving to a bigger home is not in your plans. A basement or garage renovation is also a great way to adapt to changing circumstances, such as an adult child returning home after college as he or she figures out next steps.

That all falls under the umbrella of practical considerations. But basements (and many garages) are also ideal for pure fun spaces. Something like an over-the-top game room complete with a pool table, pinball machine, and wet bar. Or how about a Hollywood-rivaling home theater focused on that 85-inch TV you've been coveting? The acoustics in many basements make the space cinema-worthy.

However, it doesn't have to be an extreme redo to be a life changer. A garage can be the perfect man cave or she grotto, attached but apart from the main structure and isolated enough to remain a private sanctuary.

Realizing any of that potential involves first dealing with crucial basic issues like proper moisture mitigation, air flow and quality, codes, and effective lighting. All of those are well covered in the sections that follow, including current gold-standard practices and up-to-date information.

Later sections describe creating rooms that capture your imagination and desires. Ultimately, whether your blank slate lies down a flight of stairs or at the top of your driveway, this book will help you exploit it to create the space of your dreams.

Gallery of Magnificent Basements + Garages

Basements

Go blond to accentuate details. Blond wood is an ideal choice for kitchen and other basement cabinetry. Here the bright, fresh look is supported by multiple light sources and reflective surfaces. All are great choices for a traditionally light-starved location.

A large basement can be an ideal space for an in-law or guest apartment. The isolation of the space lends itself to a room, or rooms, separate from the main house floor plan. Better yet, it is fairly easy to tap into existing services and create a luxurious space, like the one here. A plumbed kitchen, and a wired family room and bedrooms makes this a comfortable, useful, and quiet space. Details like granite countertops, wood plank flooring, and elegant cabinetry throughout create a stylish space.

Design for maximum light in your basement, regardless of use. These spacious, underground rooms use glass partition walls between the home gym, game room, and spare sleeping quarters. Not only do the translucent barriers allow a maximum of light to penetrate the space, the glass walls look sleek and sophisticated.

Choose a focal area for a multifaceted basement design. This walk-out basement has been transformed into separate living quarters. But whether you're entering from upstairs or outside, the kitchen is the centerpiece. It provides a visual anchor to the suite and a gathering place for residents and visitors alike.

Supersize your fantasy space. If you have a large, unused basement, you can reimagine it as an adult playground—the dream man or woman cave. This ultimate recreational space includes a curvy tiered ceiling, multilayered lighting plan, and the icing on the cake—a two-lane bowling alley!

Bring the popcorn for your new home theater. A luxurious home theater continues to be one of the most popular renovations for basements across the country. Although it looks like something out of a Beverly Hills mansion, this cinephile's dream room is achievable for most any homeowner. In this case, a big-screen projection set-up is complemented by an awe-inspiring LED-lighting scheme that includes stars in the artificial night sky of a tray ceiling.

Have a home theater . . . and even more. With today's flat-screen technology, there's no reason you can't have a stunning home theater worthy of any major motion picture, without dedicating the whole room to that function. Here a projector-screen home entertainment system is incorporated into a larger living room design. The light behind the cityscape art can be turned off as necessary for movie-watching. This way the TV doesn't steal attention from the chic interior design when the homeowner is socializing or enjoying some quiet down time in an opulent environment.

Add showcase features to up a basement's "wow" factor. A large basement like this can easily transform into a dynamic space with some thoughtful additions to draw the eye and delight occupants. Here a mirrored tray ceiling expands the spacious feeling of the basement, and a pink-hued rock gas fireplace grabs attention whether it's lit or not.

Keep it cozy. Where basement space is fairly modest, homey, emotive décor can feel absolutely perfect. Here what could otherwise be a bit of a dim basement is kept light with bright white ceilings, and pale pastel wall hues. The focus, though, is on relaxing in simple, enjoyable comfort.

Garages: The Aboveground Basement

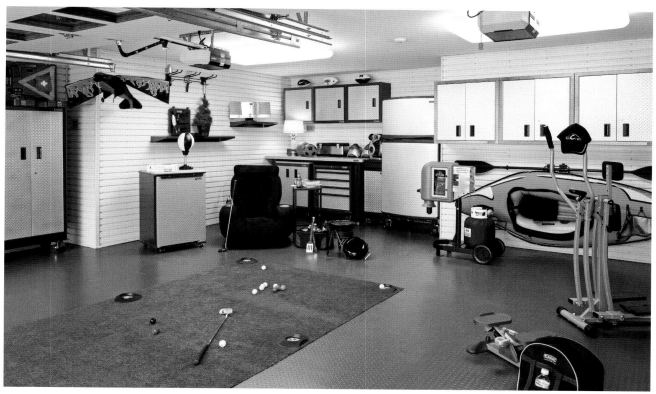

Get your sports on. The open nature of any large garage lends itself to a gym-like atmosphere. This sparkling space is finished with a rubber roll flooring that would also work in a basement, and bright fluorescent lighting to keep details crisp to the eye. The clean look and durable flooring are ideal for a home putting green, and workout equipment, with an alcove dedicated to a miniworkshop including abundant tool storage.

Exploit the space in a way that makes sense. Because it has more ready access to the outside and the yard than most basements would, it's only logical to turn to a garage for storage of tools and outdoor accessories, like this mountain bike. There are a wealth of manufactured supply storage units for just about every conceivable item you might want to store in a garage or in a basement.

Roadmap to Successful Conversions

Precise and thoughtful floor plans are key to envisioning your ideal basement or garage space and in actually crafting that space to your satisfaction. Although you can sketch a floor plan by hand, precision takes a lot of effort and time. A computer-aided design (CAD) home-design program allows you to capture the space with exacting measurements, and offers a wealth of other benefits as well. These programs are relatively inexpensive, easy to use, and can head off a lot of problems.

Simply input the dimensions of the space and the program will create a 2D floor plan. You can easily add the location of services such as a vertical waste stack or HVAC unit. Interior walls can be created with a couple of clicks and moved just as easily. The plans created are generally accepted by building departments across the country.

However, most home-design CAD programs offer so much more. They usually include a library of furniture shapes so you can position different pieces around the space to see what works best. Some programs even allow you to render the layout in a 3D, rotatable form. This is where you can get a sense of what it will actually be like to spend time in the space, how different rooms relate to each other, and where potential trouble spots appear.

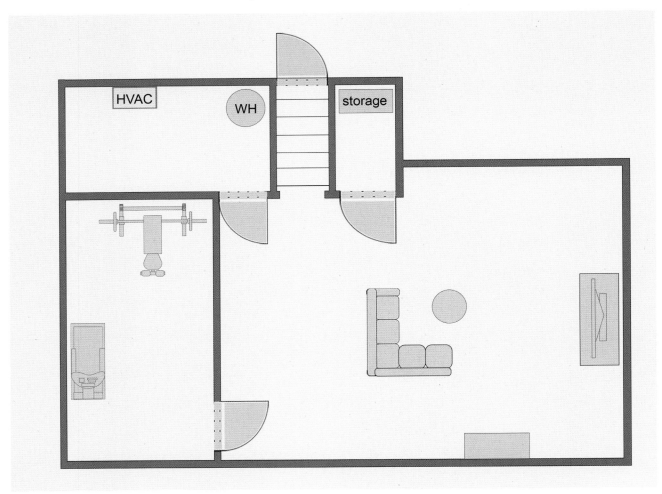

This standard floor plan lays out the space in a rectangular basement, leaving room for essential utilities and access to the HVAC and electrical systems. Created digitally with a CAD program, it is simple, clear, concise and acceptable to most local building departments.

A fully featured in-law suite like this requires a great deal of thought in how you'll use the space and how the rooms relate to one another. Obviously several of these rooms could have been placed in different areas of the floor plan. Thinking through the right position for everything is key to long-term happiness with your basement or garage renovation and is made that much easier with computer-aided design.

A 3D version of the floor plan above brings crucial elements to life. This type of computer-generated model allows you to set or change flooring type, paint color, features like mirrors and TVs, and much more. It is essentially one step shy of being able to walk through the finished space before it is finished.

REMODELING BASICS

Evaluating + Planning

If you've read this far, it's probably apparent that your unfinished basement or garage represents a fantastic opportunity. Having seen examples, you've been able to winnow your choices down to exactly the type of space you would most use and enjoy. You can clearly envision the style and function of your renovated basement or garage. Now what?

The journey from an unfinished or partially finished space to a useful and enjoyable one starts with detail-oriented planning. When tackling a basement or garage renovation, keep in mind that you won't have the luxury you might have with other rooms. If the design of a bump-out in a standard room addition needs to be changed, it's usually just a matter of adjusting measurements. There is no such luxury in the fixed features and square footage of a basement or in the set footprint of a garage slab.

That's why any basement or garage project starts with a commonsense evaluation of the usable footprint and physical environment. This section aids you in making that assessment. From that starting point, success becomes a matter of taking the right steps in the right order. That normally involves a trip to the local building or zoning department and a sober consideration of the structural elements—such as the integrity of foundation, walls, and the presence or absence of moisture.

These preliminary details are not the most exciting parts of creating your dream space, but they are essential first steps toward a successful, problem-free basement or garage renovation.

In this chapter:

- Evaluating Your Basement or Garage
- Remodeling Codes + Practices
- Planning Your Project

Evaluating Your Basement or Garage

Measure clearances from pipes and ductwork to walls and ceilings. Any obstructions that are not contained within the stud or joist cavities will need to be moved or isolated in framed chases or soffits.

Begin your evaluation by measuring from the floor joists to the bottom of the floor above. Most building codes require habitable rooms to have a finished ceiling height of seven and a half feet, measured from the finished floor to the lowest part of the finished ceiling. However, obstructions, such as beams, soffits, and pipes, (spaced at least four feet on center) can usually hang down six inches below that height. Hallways and bathrooms typically need at least seven-foot ceilings.

While it's impractical to add headroom in a basement, there are some ways of working around the requirements. Ducts and pipes can often be moved, and beams and other obstructions can be incorporated into walls or hidden in closets or other uninhabitable spaces. Also, some codes permit lower ceiling heights in rooms with specific purposes such as recreation. If headroom is a problem, talk to the local building department before you give up on your dream room.

A well-built basement or garage is structurally sound and provides plenty of support for finished space, but before you cover up the walls, floor, and ceiling, check for potential problems. Inspect the masonry carefully. Large cracks may indicate a shifting around the foundation; severely bowed or out-of-plumb walls may be structurally unsound. Small cracks usually cause moisture problems rather than structural woes, but they should be sealed to prevent further cracking. Contact an engineer or foundation contractor for help with foundation problems. If you have an older home, you may find sagging floor joists, rafters, or even a compromised garage roof overhead or rotted wood posts or beams; any defective wood framing will have to be reinforced or replaced.

Mechanicals are another important consideration. The locations of water heaters, pipes, wiring, circuit boxes, furnaces, and ductwork can have a significant impact on the cost and difficulty of your project. Can you plan around components or will they have to be moved? Is there enough headroom to install a suspended ceiling so mechanicals can remain accessible? Or, will you have to reroute pipes and ducts to increase headroom? Electricians and Heating Ventilation and Air Conditioning (HVAC) contractors can assess your systems and suggest modifications.

How to Evaluate Your Basement or Garage

Trace plumbing lines and note locations of shutoff valves on supply lines, which are natural points for adding new pipes or redirecting old pipes. If you are considering a bathroom or kitchen addition, also trace drain lines back to the main drain stack, and take measurements to determine if adding new drain lines is feasible.

Evaluate headroom, paying particular attention to ductwork that is mounted below the bottoms of the floor joists. In many cases, you can reroute the ductwork so it runs in the joist cavity.

Look for asbestos insulation, usually found on hot air supply ducts from the furnace. Asbestos removal is dangerous and closely regulated, but it in many cases you can do it yourself if you follow the right proscriptions. Check with your local building department or waste management authority for more information on asbestos abatement in your area.

Identify sources of standing water and visible leaks. If water comes into the basement on a regular basis through the foundation walls or floor, you'll definitely need to correct the problem before you begin your basement project. See pages 32 to 39.

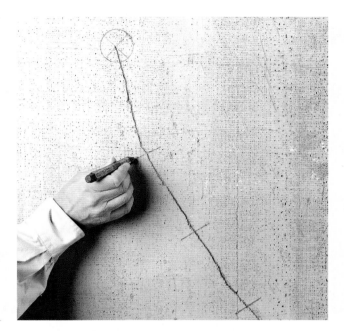

Inspect foundation wall cracks to see if they are stable. Draw marks across the crack and take measurements at the marks. Compare measurements for a few months to see if the crack is widening. If the crack is stable you can repair it. If it is moving, contact a structural engineer and resolve the problem before you begin your remodeling project.

Probe small cracks in poured concrete walls and floors with a cold chisel to evaluate the condition of the concrete. If the concrete flakes off easily, keep probing until you get to solid concrete. If the crack and loose material extend more than 1" or so into the wall, contact a structural engineer.

Check the mortar joints on concrete block foundation walls. Some degradation is normal, but if gaps wider than ¼" have formed, you should have the wall repaired before you begin building.

Check for bowing in basement walls. Water pressure in the ground often causes concrete walls to bow inward over time. As long as the amount of bowing is less than 1" or 2" and the bowing is not active, you can usually address the problem by furring out from the wall with a framed wall.

Testing Basement + Garage Conditions

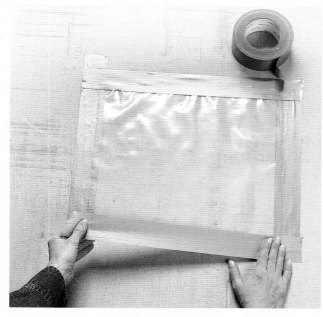

Test concrete floors for moisture seepage by taping a piece of plastic to the floor and leaving it in place for a day. If moisture is entering the basement through the floor, you will see it accumulating on the underside of the plastic.

Test concrete foundation walls for moisture and condensation. Tape a small square of aluminum foil to the wall and leave it in place for a day. If the outside surface of the foil becomes wet, you have a condensation problem, which is normally corrected by installing a dehumidifer. If the surface against the wall becomes wet, you have a seepage problem (see pages 32 to 39).

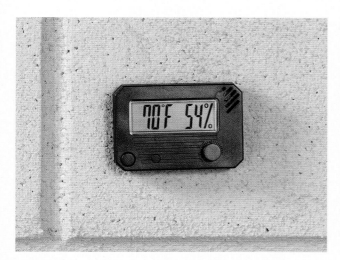

Test humidity. A relative humidity of 30% to 40% is considered ideal, but can be hard to achieve in a basement, where the naturally cooler temperatures mean that relative humidity is higher to start with. Use a hygrometer to measure relative humidity in your basement. If it is more than 50%, you will probably need to include the installation of a high-capacity dehumidifier in your remodeling plans.

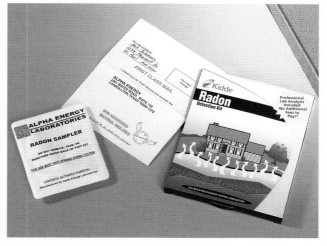

Test for excessive radon. Radon is an odorless, colorless, radioactive gas that can enter up through basement floors and accumulate, posing a health hazard. Some smoke detectors will detect radon, but only if it is already at dangerous levels. To determine if you have a potential radon problem, you can purchase a fairly expensive digital radon detector, or you can buy an inexpensive home detection kit available at hardware stores. You simply take an air sample with the kit collector and mail the sample to the laboratory. In most cases, you'll receive a report with recommendations in a week or two.

A new, high-efficiency water heater that's sized for your usage is a good investment.

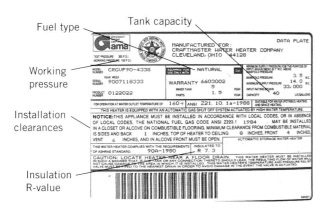

Evaluate your water heater to determine if it has enough capacity to support a bathroom, especially if your project will include a bathtub or shower. If you already run out of hot water on occasion (or if your current water heater is more than 7 to 10 years old), consider upgrading.

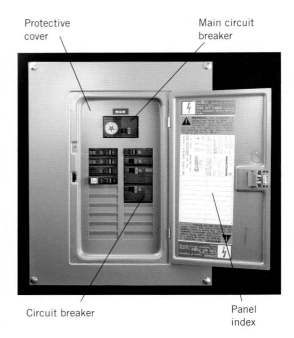

Check your main electrical service panel to gauge if there is enough available capacity for you to add the additional electrical circuits your remodeling will require. Start by looking for unused slots that are still covered with metal knockout plates. If there are several available, that's a good sign that you may be able to expand. But to know for sure, you'll need to calculate the current load your home is using and compare it to the maximum capacity. You can find the information for making these calculations in any wiring book or on the internet. Or, have an electrician make the assessment for you. Here are general guidelines for new circuits:

Small bathroom: One 15-amp light circuit and one dedicated 20-amp small appliance circuit (GFCI protected).

Bathroom suite: One 15-amp light circuit; one 20-amp small appliance circuit (GFCI protected); dedicated 30- or 40-amp, 240-volt circuit for jetted bath or sauna; dedicated 20-amp, 240-volt circuit for electric baseboard heaters (up to 16 ft.).

Bedroom: One 15-amp light circuit; One 15- or 20-amp receptacle circuit.

Home office/home theater: One 15-amp light circuit; One 20-amp receptacle circuit with surge protection; structured wiring or home networking cabling as required.

Measure the distance from areas where you are considering installing plumbing drains to the main drain stack. The new branch drain line needs to slope down to the main stack at a minimum rate of ¼" per ft. The slope is created by running the drain line through the existing floor and tying into the main stack below floor level (see pages 192 to 196) or by elevating the fixture. In a garage, you may be able to tie into a main stack without excavating the slab, depending on the location of the new room and the existing lines.

BASEMENT CONSTRUCTION

Modern basements vary somewhat in how they are constructed, but most have concrete or concrete block foundation walls that are poured on footings and support the walls above them. The joists for the first floor are supported on the ends by sills that are fastened to the tops of the foundation walls, which they share with rim joists. The joists are usually supported in the center by a beam that is in turn supported by posts and beams or by a load-bearing wall that runs straight through the house. The bearing wall rests on an area of the floor that has been reinforced with a footing.

If the house is built on sloping terrain, it is common to have a walkout door so the basement area may be entered at grade level on the low end of the slope. In addition to making access easier, the walkout door (often a sliding patio door) allows plenty of natural light into the basement.

In some older homes, the basement foundation walls do not bear weight. You can usually identify these by the fact that the walls extend only a short distance below grade, and are often set back from a ledge of buttressed earth. In these basements, the bulk of the bearing work is done by posts and beams.

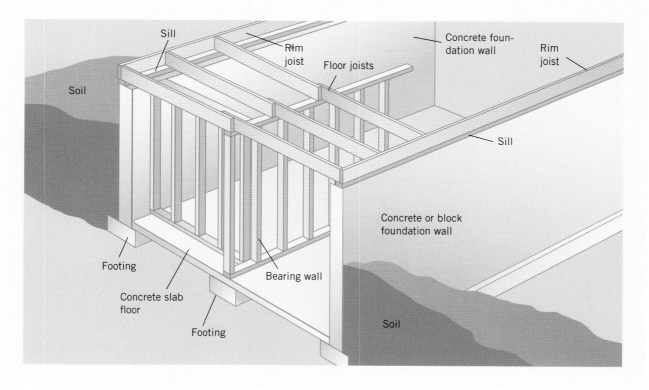

Remodeling Codes & Practices

Converting a basement or garage into livable space involves conquering a set of challenges that are unique to the construction. This is why basement and garage remodeling and finishing are regulated by codes and practices that differ from other rooms. Many of the standards relate to the constant threat posed by water runoff and moisture that percolates in through the adjoining soil. Some deal with air quality in a cool environment with high relative humidity that favors mold growth. Egress (the ability to get in and out easily) is very important in basements—you can't simply jump out a window if the main entryway is blocked. Even gravity can work against you where draining water may require assistance to be efficiently removed.

Building codes distinguish between habitable space and nonliving space. All habitable rooms must have a footprint of at least seventy square feet (sf) with at least one wall that's seven feet or longer. The exception is a kitchen, which can be as small as fifty square feet in some instances. However, it should be noted that a small bedroom is usually considered to be in the one hundred square foot to one hundred fifty square foot range, so you should consider a seventy square foot bedroom only under extremely tight conditions. Minimum ceiling height is seven feet, with some exceptions. Beams or ductwork may not drop down more than six inches from the ceiling.

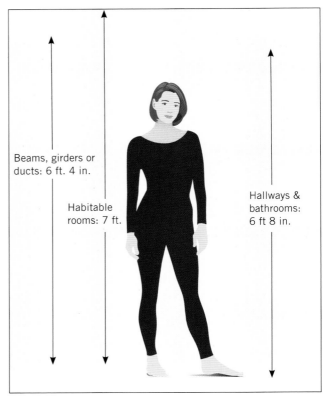

Beams, girders or ducts: 6 ft. 4 in.

Habitable rooms: 7 ft.

Hallways & bathrooms: 6 ft 8 in.

Headroom is often limited by beams, ducts, pipes, and other elements. Typical minimums for ceiling height are shown here: 7 ft. for habitable rooms; 6 ft. 8 in. for bathrooms and hallways; 6 ft. 4in. for obstructions such as girders or ducts.

ADDITIONAL CODE REQUIREMENTS

Permanently installed appliances, such as furnaces and water heaters must be fully accessible for inspection, service, repair, and replacement. A dedicated furnace room must have a door at least wide and large enough for passage of the furnace. There should be a minimum area of clear space for maintenance access. Check with your local building department for combustion air supply requirements.

Clothes dryers must exhaust to the exterior.

Bathrooms without natural ventilation must have artificial ventilation of at least 50 cu ft. per minute intermittent, or 20 cfm constant that is vented to the exterior. Ventilation in half baths (no tub or shower) can exhaust into the attic in some areas.

Electrical service panels may not be located in bathrooms or over stairs.

GFCI receptacles or circuits are required in bathrooms, unfinished spaces, and on countertops within 6 ft. of a faucet.

Receptacles are required every 6 ft. in all habitable rooms. They are also required in any wall area wider than 1 ft., laundry areas, and in any hallway longer than 10 ft.

Habitable rooms, storage room, utility room, hallway, or staircase must have at least one switch-operated light fixture. Habitable rooms must also have an amount of window glass area equal to at least 8% of the area of the floor. At least half of the window area must be openable for unobstructed ventilation. Artificial lights and mechanical ventilation may be substituted under some conditions.

Unfinished areas must have windows with an unobstructed ventilation area equal to 1% of the floor area.

Egress Window Considerations

If your home has an unfinished or partially finished basement, it's an enticing and sensible place to expand your practical living space. Another bedroom or two, a game room, or maybe a spacious home office are all possibilities. However, unless your basement has a walk-out doorway, you'll need to add an egress window to make your new living space meet most building codes. That's because the International Residential Code (IRC) requires two forms of escape for every living space—an exit door and a window large enough for you to climb out of or for an emergency responder to enter.

Code mandates that a below-ground egress window will have a minimum opening area of at least 5.7 square feet. There are stipulations about how this open area can be proportioned: The window must be at least 20 inches wide and 24 inches high when open. Additionally, the installed window's sill height must be within 44 inches of the basement floor to permit easy escape. Typical basement windows do not meet these requirements. A large egress window requires an oversized window well. The well must be at least 36 inches wide and project 36 inches or more from the foundation. If the window well is deeper than 44 inches, it must have a fixed ladder for escape.

What does this all mean for the ambitious do-it-yourselfer? The good news is that if you've got the nerve to cut an oversized opening in your home's foundation, and you don't mind spending some quality time with a shovel, installing a basement egress window is a manageable project. Here's a case where careful planning, a building permit, and some help can save you considerable money over hiring a contractor to do the work. For a complete step-by-step egress window and well installation, see pages 156 to 161. Contact your local building department to learn more about specific egress requirements that apply to your area.

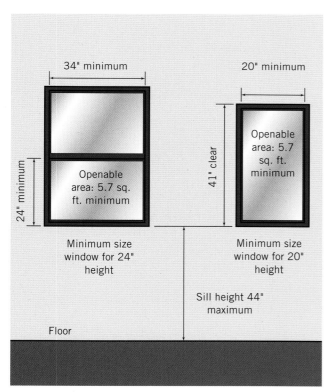

In order to satisfy building codes for egress, a basement window must have a minimum opening of 5.7 sq. ft. through one sash, with at least 20" of clear width and 24" of clear height. Casement, double-hung, and sliding window styles can be used, as long as their dimensions for width and height meet these minimum requirements.

Egress window wells must be at least 36" wide and project 36" from the foundation. Those deeper than 44" must have a means of escape, such as a tiered design that forms steps or an attached ladder. Drainage at the bottom of the well should extend down to the foundation footing drain, with pea gravel used as the drainage material.

Planning Your Project

After you've evaluated your basement or garage and have determined that the space is usable, the next step is to plan the construction project. Having a complete construction plan enables you to view the entire project at a glance. It helps you identify potential problems, provides a schedule, and establishes a logical order of steps. Without a construction plan, it's easier to make costly errors, like closing up a wall with wallboard before the rough-ins are inspected.

The general steps shown here follow a typical construction sequence. Your plan likely will differ at several points, but thinking through each of these steps will help you create a complete schedule.

1. Contact the building department and discuss your project with a building official. Find out what codes apply in your area and how to obtain the applicable permits. Explain how much of the work you plan to do yourself. In some states, plumbing, electrical, and HVAC work must be done by licensed professionals. Also determine what types of drawings you'll need to get permits and what costs will be.

2. Design the space. Take measurements, make sketches, and test different layouts—find out what works and what doesn't. Consider all the necessary elements, such as headroom, lighting, mechanicals, and make sure everything adheres to local building codes.

3. Draw floor plans. Most remodels can follow a simple set of plans that you can draw yourself. Plans should include dimensions of rooms, doors, and windows; and locations of all plumbing fixtures and HVAC equipment; electrical fixtures, receptacles, and switches; and closets, counters, and other built-in features.

4. Hire contractors. If you're getting help with your project, it's best to find and hire the contractors early in the process. You may need certain contractors to pull their own permits. To avoid problems, make sure all contractors know exactly what work they are being hired to do and what work you will be doing yourself. Always check contractor's references and make sure they're licensed and insured. Make sure you get a detailed contract to review, with relevant dates and expectations spelled out.

5. Get the permits. Take your drawings, notes, and any required documents to the building department, and obtain the permits for your project. Find out what work needs to be inspected and when to call for inspections. This is a critical step, because the permit process is required by law.

6. Make major structural and mechanical changes. Prepare the space for finishing by completing structural work and building new stairs, if necessary. Move mechanical elements and re-route major service lines. Complete rough-ins that must happen before the framing, such as adding ducts, installing under-floor drains, and replacing old plumbing.

7. Frame the rooms. Build the floors, walls, and ceilings that establish your new rooms. In most cases, the floor will come first; however, you should rough-in service lines and insulate for soundproofing before installing the subfloor. Next come the walls. Cover foundation walls, and build partition walls and knee walls. Build the rough openings for windows and doors. Enlarge existing window openings or cut new ones for egress windows. Install the windows.

8. Complete the rough-ins. Run DWV (drain, waste, and vent) and water and gas supply pipes. Install electrical boxes, and run the wiring. Complete the HVAC rough-ins. Build soffits to enclose new service lines.

9. Insulate. Insulate the walls, ceilings, and pipes for weatherizing, soundproofing, and fireblocking. Add vapor barriers if required by local code.

10. Finish the walls and ceilings. If you're installing wallboard, do the ceilings first, then the walls. Tape and finish the wallboard. Install other finish treatments.

11. Add the finishing touches. Complete finish carpentry, such as installing doors, moldings and other woodwork, cabinets, and built-in shelving, and lay the floor coverings.

12. Make the final connections. Install the plumbing fixtures and complete the drain and supply hookups. Make electrical connections, and install all fixtures, devices, and appliances. Get the final inspection and approval.

RECOMMENDED CLEARANCES

A bathroom should be planned with enough approach space and clearance room to allow a wheelchair or walker user to enter and turn around easily. The guidelines for approach spaces and clearances shown here include some ADA guidelines and recommendations from universal design specialists.

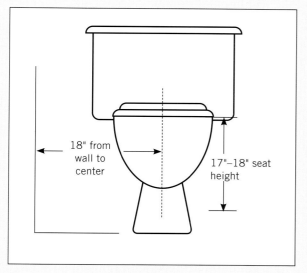

18" from wall to center

17"–18" seat height

Toilet

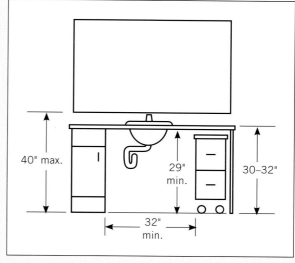

40" max.

29" min.

30–32"

32" min.

Sink & Vanity

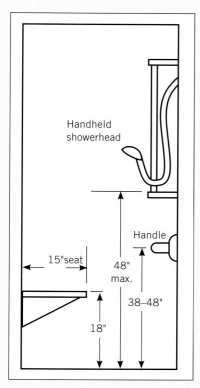

Handheld showerhead

Handle

15"seat

48" max.

38–48"

18"

Shower

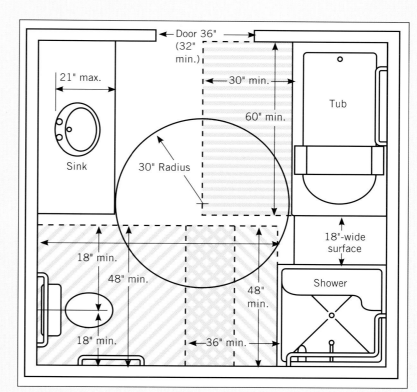

Door 36" (32" min.)

21" max.

Sink

30" Radius

30" min.

60" min.

Tub

18"-wide surface

Shower

18" min.

48" min.

18" min.

36" min.

48" min.

Floor Plan

Improving Basement Environments

Before you get down to the actual building of rooms, you need to make any environmental upgrades that are necessary for the comfort, safety, and livability of the room. Now is the time to deal with water or moisture problems, heating and cooling requirements, ventilation needs, and upgrades to the wiring or plumbing systems that are needed to support additional finished living space. Ultimately, the success of your rec room or laundry room or guest bedroom depends on how conscientiously you manage the environmental changes.

As you prepare the basement for construction, keep a few fundamental guidelines in mind. Each of these is addressed in greater detail in this chapter.

• Do not insulate exterior basement walls on the interior side.
• Do not install vapor barriers on the interior side of basement walls (unless required by local codes).
• Leave airspace between furred basement walls and exterior walls.
• Make sure all moisture infiltration problems are addressed by eliminating the source or, if that is not possible, by installing a sump pump or other mechanical means for removing water.

In this chapter:
• Controlling Moisture
• Controlling Pests
• Insulating Basements
• Improving Heating + Cooling
• Upgrading Ventilation
• Adding Electrical Circuits

Controlling Moisture

Basement moisture can destroy your efforts to create a functional living space. Over time, even small amounts of moisture can rot framing, turn wallboard to mush, and promote the growth of mold and mildew. Before proceeding with your basement project, you must deal with any moisture issues. The good news is that moisture problems can be resolved, often very easily.

Basement moisture appears in two forms: condensation and seepage. Condensation comes from airborne water vapor that turns to water when it contacts cold surfaces. Vapor sources include humid outdoor air, poorly ventilated appliances, damp walls, and water released from concrete. Seepage is water that enters the basement by infiltrating cracks in the foundation or by leeching through masonry, which is naturally porous. Often caused by ineffective exterior drainage, seepage comes from rain or groundwater that collects around the foundation or from a rising water table.

If you have a wet basement, you'll see evidence of moisture problems. Typical signs include peeling paint, white residue on masonry (called efflorescence), mildew stains, sweaty windows and pipes, rusted appliance feet, rotted wood near the floor, buckled floor tile, and strong mildew odor.

To reduce condensation, run a high-capacity dehumidifier in the basement. Insulate cold-water pipes to prevent condensate drippage, and make sure your dryer and other appliances have vents running to the outside. Extending central air conditioning service to the basement can help reduce vapor during warm, humid months.

Crawlspaces can also promote condensation, as warm, moist air enters through vents and meets cooler interior air. Crawlspace ventilation is a source of ongoing debate, and there's no universal method that applies to all climates. It's best to ask the local building department for advice on this matter.

Solutions for preventing seepage range from simple do-it-yourself projects to expensive, professional jobs requiring excavation and foundation work. Since it's often difficult to determine the source of seeping water, it makes sense to try some common cures before calling in professional help. If the simple measures outlined here don't correct your moisture problems, you

Repairing cracks restores the integrity of concrete foundation walls that leak, but it is often only a temporary fix. Selecting an appropriate repair product and doing careful preparation will make the repair more long lasting. A hydraulic concrete repair product like the one seen here is perfect for basement wall repair because it actually hardens from contact with water.

must consider more extensive action. Serious water problems are typically handled by installing footing drains or sump pump systems. Footing drains are installed around the foundation's perimeter, near the footing, and they drain out to a distant area of the yard. These usually work in conjunction with waterproof coatings on the exterior side of the foundation walls. Sump systems use an interior underslab drainpipe to collect water in a pit, and water is ejected outside by an electric sump pump.

Installing a new drainage system is expensive and must be done properly. Adding a sump system involves breaking up the concrete floor along the basement's perimeter, digging a trench, and laying a perforated drainpipe in a bed of gravel. After the sump pit is installed, the floor is patched with new concrete. Installing a footing drain is far more complicated. This involves digging out the foundation, installing gravel and drainpipe, and waterproofing the foundation walls. A footing drain is considered a last-resort measure.

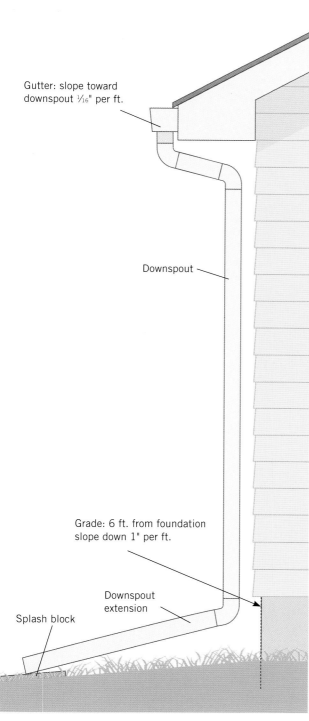

Gutter: slope toward downspout ¹⁄₁₆" per ft.

Downspout

Grade: 6 ft. from foundation slope down 1" per ft.

Downspout extension

Splash block

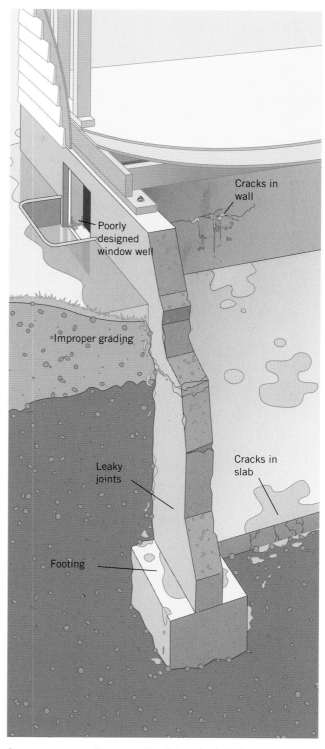

Cracks in wall

Poorly designed window well

Improper grading

Leaky joints

Cracks in slab

Footing

Improve your gutter system and foundation grade to prevent rainwater and snowmelt from flooding your basement. Keep gutters clean and straight. Make sure there's a downspout for every 50 ft. of roof eave, and extend downspouts at least 8 ft. from the foundation. Build up the grade around the foundation so that it carries water away from the house.

Common causes of basement moisture include improper grading around the foundation, inadequate or faulty gutter systems, condensation, cracks in foundation walls, leaky joints between structural elements, and poorly designed window wells. More extensive problems include large cracks in the foundation, damaged or missing drain tiles, a high water table, or the presence of underground streams. Often, a combination of factors is at fault.

How to Seal Cracks in a Foundation Wall

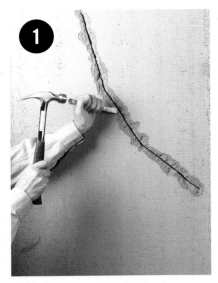

1

To repair a stable crack, chisel cut a keyhole cut that's wider at the base then at the surface, and no more than ½" deep. Clean out the crack with a wire brush.

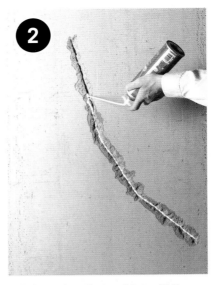

2

To help seal against moisture, fill the crack with expanding insulating foam, working from bottom to top.

3

Mix hydraulic cement according to the manufacturer's instructions, then trowel it into the crack, working from the bottom to top. Apply cement in layers no more than ¼" thick, until the patch is slightly higher than the surrounding area. Feather cement with the trowel until it's even with the surface. Allow to dry thoroughly.

 # How to Skim-Coat a Foundation Wall

1

Resurface heavily cracked masonry walls with a water-resistant masonry coating such as surface bonding cement. Clean and dampen the walls according to the coating manufacturer's instructions, then fill large cracks and holes with the coating. Finally, plaster a ¼"-layer of the coating on the walls using a square-end trowel. Specially formulated heavy-duty masonry coatings are available for very damp conditions.

2

Scratch the surface with a paintbrush cleaner or a homemade scratching tool after the coating has set up for several hours. After 24 hours, apply a second, smooth coat. Mist the wall twice a day for three days as the coating cures.

Preventing Moisture in Basements

BRUSH-ON WATERPROOFING SEALANT

Epoxy waterproofing sealers are thick, paint-like materials that are brushed onto surfaces like basement foundation walls to make them watertight. First used on water tanks, ponds, and pools, these products are self-curing, easy to use, and designed to resist hydrostatic pressure. This makes them a good choice to coat basement walls in which large or small cracks have been repaired.

Most epoxy sealers are available with a variety of tints. This allows you to color an exposed foundation wall to match the rest of the space. When not tinted, the material cures clear.

Waterproofing paint is less effective than epoxy coatings, but is a decorative option that will keep a wall relatively water resistant. If you choose this option, make sure the label specifies that the product is meant for use on basement walls.

Clean your gutters and patch any holes. Make sure the gutters slope toward the downspouts at about 1/16" per ft. Add downspout extensions and splash blocks to keep roof runoff at least 8 ft. away from the foundation.

Cover window wells that will otherwise allow water into a basement. Covering them with removable plastic is the easiest way to keep them dry. Covers on egress window wells must be easily removed from inside. If you prefer to leave wells uncovered, add a gravel layer and a drain to the bottom of the well. Clean the well regularly to remove moisture-heavy debris.

Drainage Solution: How to Regrade

Establish the drainage slope. The yard around your house should slant away from the house at a minimum slope of ¼" per ft. for at least 10 ft. Till the soil or add new soil around the house perimeter. Drive a wood stake next to the house and another 10 ft. out. Tie a level mason's string between the stakes, and then move the string down at least ¼" at the end away from the house, establishing your minimum slope.

Redistribute the soil with a steel garden rake so the grade follows the slope line. Add topsoil at the high end if needed. Do not excavate near the end of the slope to accommodate the grade. The goal is to build up the yard to create runoff.

Use a grading rake to smooth out the soil so it slopes at an even rate. Drive additional stakes and tie off slope lines as necessary.

Tamp the soil with a hand tamper or plate compactor. Fill in any dips that occur with fresh dirt. Lay sod or plant grass or groundcover immediately.

Drainage Solution: How to Install a Dry Well

A dry well is a simple way to channel excess water out of low-lying or water-laden areas, such as the ground beneath a gutter downspout. It usually consists of a buried drain tile running from a catch basin positioned at the problem spot, to a collection container some distance away. In the project shown here, a perforated plastic drain tile carries water from the catch basin to a plastic trashcan that has been punctured and filled with stones. The runoff water percolates into the soil as it makes its way along the drain tile and through the dry well.

Set a length of perforated drain tile on the gravel running the full length of the trench. If the trench starts at a downspout, position a grated catch basin directly beneath the downspout and attach the end of the drain tile to the outlet port.

Dig a trench (10" wide, 14" deep) from the area where the water collects to the catch basin location, sloping the trench 2" per 8 ft. Line the trench with landscape fabric and then add a 1" layer of gravel on top of the fabric.

 ## DRY WELLS FOR DRAINAGE

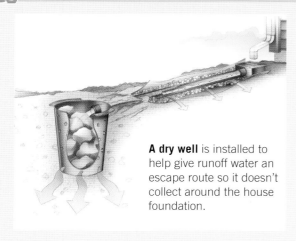

A dry well is installed to help give runoff water an escape route so it doesn't collect around the house foundation.

Install the dry well by digging a hole that's big enough to hold a plastic trash can. Drill 1" holes through the sides and bottom of the can every 4" to 6". Also cut an access hole at the top of the can for the drain tile. Set the can in the hole and insert the free end of the tile. Backfill dirt over the tile and trench and plant grass or cover with sod.

Drainage Solution: How to Install a Sump Pump

If water continues to accumulate in your basement despite all your efforts at sealing your basement walls, installing a sump pump may be your only option for resolving the problem. Permanently located in a pit that you dig beneath your basement floor, the sump pump automatically kicks in whenever enough water accumulates in the pit to trigger the pump float. The water is then pumped out of the basement through a pipe that runs through the rim joist of the house.

Because you'll be digging well beneath the basement floor, make certain there is no sewer pipe or water supply pipe in the digging area. Contact a plumber if you do not know for sure that the area is clear.

The purpose of a sump pump is to collect and remove water that accumulates beneath your basement floor (usually due to a high water table) before it can be drawn or forced up into the basement. The most effective sump installations have drain tile running around the entire perimeter of the house and channeling water to the pump pit. This system can be created as a retrofit job, but it is a major undertaking best left to a pro.

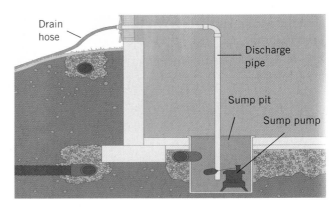

A submersible sump pump is installed in a pit beneath a basement floor to pump water out before it seeps up into the basement.

 ## How to Install a Sump Pump

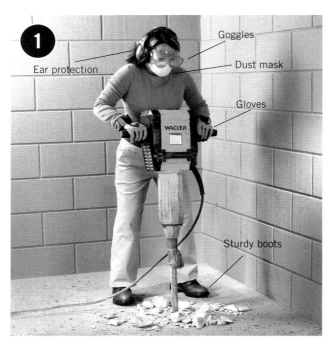

Dig the sump pit. Start by finding the lowest point of the floor (or the spot where water typically accumulates) that is at least 8" from a foundation wall. Outline an area that's about 6" wider than the pit liner all around. Remove the concrete in this area. Basement floors are typically 3" to 4" thick, so renting an electric jackhammer is a good idea.

Install the pit liner after digging a hole for it in the granular material under the floor. The hole should be a few inches wider than the liner. Remove the excavated material right away. Add gravel to the bottom of the hole as needed to bring the liner level with the top of its rim at floor level.

Pack the liner in place by pouring ½" gravel around it. Add a 1" base of gravel and then mix concrete to patch the floor. Trowel the concrete around the rim with a float so the patch is level and smooth.

Prepare the sump pump for installation. Thread a PVC adapter fitting onto the pump outlet, and then solvent glue a PVC standpipe to the adapter. The standpipe should be long enough to extend about 1 ft. past the liner rim when the pump is set on the bottom of the liner.

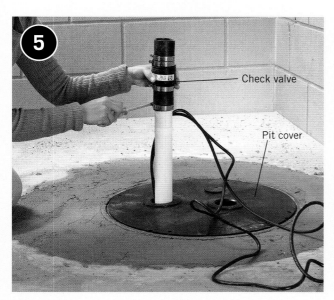

Check valve

Pit cover

Attach a check valve to the top of the standpipe to prevent the backflow of water into the pump pit. Solvent weld another riser to fit into the top of the check valve and run upward to a point level with the rim joist, where the discharge tube will exit the basement.

Drill a hole in the rim joist for the discharge tube and finish routing the drainpipe out through the rim joist. Caulk around the tube on both the interior and exterior sides. On the exterior, attach an elbow fitting to the discharge tube and run drainpipe down from the elbow. Place a splash block beneath the drainpipe to direct water away from the house. Plug the pump in to a GFCI-protected receptacle.

Controlling Pests

A typical basement offers everything a pest could ask for: it's cool and damp with plenty of hiding places and ample food sources. Insects will happily invade your basement in just about any climate, typically entering through cracks in the foundation wall as well as through floor drains. In some areas, snakes are drawn to the cool climate in basements. Other invaders include vermin (mice and rats) and, perhaps the most destructive of all, termites.

The most common entry points are small holes along the foundation and sometimes next to windows and doors. These should all be filled with silicone acrylic caulk. Holes much wider than ¼" should be stuffed with caulk backer before caulking. Also fill any gaps where gas, cable, electric, water, and other services enter the house through the basement. Once you are done filling the obvious gaps, look for evidence of infestation like animal droppings or nesting materials. Remove these and check the area for any entry points that you might have missed. If the rodents persist, you can fight back with spring-loaded traps or humane traps that capture the animal so it can be released outside.

There are many hardware store products designed to help you get rid of pests inside your house. For insects in the basement, pesticide foggers are one option. These shouldn't be used around food prep areas or when anyone is in the house. The usual approach is to activate the fogger and then leave the house for a few hours. No matter which product you buy, follow the use instructions carefully.

Common roach and ant traps do capture a lot of pests but will not solve the problem unless the source from outside is eliminated. The same is true of mousetraps. If you've closed all the entry points that you can find, and you've trapped all the pests that were inside when you plugged the holes and you still have pests, then you need further help. Call a reputable exterminator.

If you have a termite problem, do not fool around with home remedies. Contact a pest control professional, who will most likely get you set up with a monitored trap system. Because termites can destroy your house (and new, more destructive breeds are proliferating quickly), don't take any chances.

Control termites by having a professionally monitored bait system installed. If you live in an area where termites are a problem, relying on home remedies is a risky gamble.

Block basement floor drains from becoming entry points by setting a tennis ball in the drain opening. The lightweight ball will cover the opening but float up enough to allow water to drain.

Pestproofing Basements

Seal the mudsill by applying caulk or expandable foam between the mudsill and the top of the foundation wall on the interior side (left photo). This is a prime entry point for crawling insects. Also check the sill area on the exterior side. Often, this is concealed by siding, but if you see any gaps fill them with caulk as well (right photo).

Caulk around dryer vents to keep pests (and water) out of the basement. For maximum protection, replace your flap-style vent outlets (inset) with a protected vent hood that keeps insects and rodents out (the warm, moist air in a dryer vent is very attractive to pests).

BASEMENT PEST GUIDE

PEST	SIGN	TREATMENT
Termites	Piles of dead insects; distinctive hollow tubes down walls	Exterminator
Mice/Rats	Droppings; pest sighting	Trap (kill or live capture)
Spiders	Webs, dead prey, spiders, black widows—black with red hourglass on abdomen	Most will vacate once you clean in preparation for construction; Consult with exterminator for black widows and brown recluse
Ants and Silverfish	Trails; insects	Spray with a natural pesticide (can spray inside and out at base of foundation)

Insulating Basements

Insulating basements is a tricky topic. In colder climates, insulation is necessary to create a livable basement room. But the practice is fraught with pitfalls that can cause a host of problems. In any case, it's essential that any moisture issues have been remedied and the environment is completely dry before installing insulation. Also keep in mind that you can install insulation on the exterior as well as the interior of a foundation wall.

Almost all of the issues surrounding basement wall insulation have to do with moisture and water vapor. How these issues affect your plans will depend a great deal on your climate, as well as on the specific characteristics of your house, your building site, and whether or not your home was built with foundation drains and a pumping system.

Basements are most often insulated from the inside because it is easier, faster, and cheaper. A typical installation would be to attach furring strips (2 × 2, 2 × 3, or 2 × 4) to the foundation wall at standard wall stud spacing, and then fill in between the strips with fiberglass insulation batts. A sheet plastic vapor barrier would then be stapled over the insulated wall prior to hanging wallcoverings (usually wallboard or paneling). Experience has shown this frequently leads to moisture buildup within the wall that encourages mold growth and has a negative impact on the indoor air quality. The building materials also tend to fail prematurely from the sustained moisture presence.

If your basement plans require that you insulate the foundation walls, make certain that the walls are dry and that any moisture problems are corrected (see previous section). Then, look first at the exterior. Because it is often unnecessary to insulate the full

Install insulation on the exterior of the wall, not the interior, whenever possible. Exterior insulation results in a warm wall that will have less of a problem with condensation. The wall also can breathe and dry out more easily if the interior side has no vapor retarder.

height of the wall, you may find that an exterior apron insulating approach is easier than you imagined. If you prefer to insulate on the inside of a foundation wall, or it's the only option, the best choice of insulation is foam board. This doesn't absorb water or provide a base for mold. It's also wise to keep the finished wall isolated from the insulation or basement wall surface, by constructing a stud wall without direct contact with the basement wall.

HIGH-EFFICIENCY UPGRADES

Replace old gas water heaters with high-efficiency models. Not only will this save money on your utilities bill, it will also keep your basement warmer. The more efficient your heater is, the less air it will require for fuel combustion, which means less fresh cold air is drawn into the basement to replace the air consumed by the appliance.

How to Insulate Basements

Install rigid foam insulation in basements, both on the exterior and the interior. Extruded polystyrene is an economical choice for larger areas, and it forms its own vapor retarding layer when properly installed and sealed. High-density polystyrene and isocyanurate are denser insulation boards with higher R-values. Isocyanurate usually has one or two foil faces. It is used to seal rim joists but is a good choice for any basement wall location.

Improve insulation and thermal seals in attics and other parts of your house to keep basements warmer in winter. By reducing the amount of warm air that escapes through the roof, you will reduce the amount of cold air that is drawn in through the openings to replace the air.

Seal furnace ducts to reduce air leakage. Use a combination of UL 181-rated duct tape (foil tape) and duct mastic. If cold-air return ducts leak, for example, they will draw air from the basement into the air supply system. As with heat loss through the attic, this will cause fresh cold air to enter the basement and lower the ambient temperature.

 ## WHAT IS A DRY WALL

When building experts warn never to insulate a wall that isn't dry, they have something very specific in mind. A wall that appears dry to the touch may not be classified as dry if it is constantly evaporating small amounts of moisture that will be blocked if you install any kind of vapor retarder (as is likely the case). A dry wall (suitable for interior insulation) is one that is superficially dry to the touch and also meets these criteria:

- Has a positive drainage system capable of removing water that accumulates from any source (this is typically in the form of a sump pump).

- The foundation wall and floor are structured to provide drainage of water away from the house, often through the use of drain tiles and footing drains.

Exterior Apron Insulation

The best way to insulate an exterior wall is by installing insulation in the apron area only, so you do not have to excavate all the way to the bottom of the wall. By adding a layer of horizontal insulation in the bottom of the trench, you can realize at least 70 percent of the energy savings of insulating the whole wall, while limiting your digging to 18 inches down and 24 inches out.

Because you will be adding width to the foundation wall by installing exterior insulation, you will need to install flashing to cover the top of the insulation layer and whatever protective wall surface you cover it with.

For the project shown here, the insulation is covered with panelized veneer siding over one-inch-thick rigid foam insulation boards. For extra protection, coat the cleaned walls with a layer of bituminous coating before installing the insulation boards.

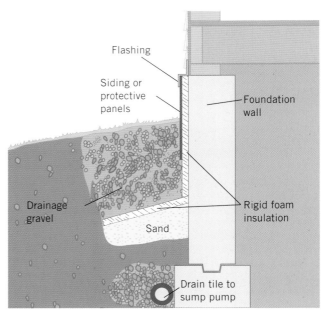

Apron insulation is an easy and effective way to make the basement more comfortable, and save energy without causing any moisture issues.

 ## How to Install Apron Insulation

Contact the local utility company to mark any power, gas, or sewer lines running under the trench area. Dig an 18" × 24" wide trench next to the wall being insulated.

Coat the wall with a layer of bituminous coating once you have cleaned it with a hose or pressure washer. The coating creates another layer of moisture protection for the basement.

Line the trench with a 2"-thick layer of coarse sand, and then strips of rigid foam insulation. The sand should slope away from the house slightly, and the insulation strips should butt up against the foundation wall.

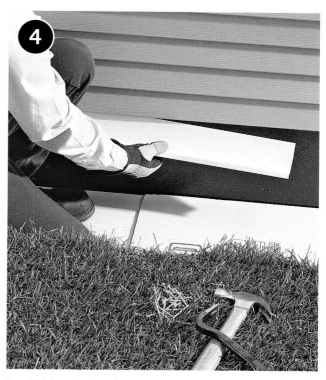

Install drip edge flashing to protect the tops of the insulation board and new siding. Pry back the bottom edge of the siding slightly and slip the flashing flange up underneath the siding. The flashing should extend out far enough to cover both layers of new material (at least 1½ to 2").

Bond strips of rigid foam insulation board to the foundation wall using a panel adhesive that is compatible with foam. Press the tops of the boards up against the drip edge flashing. When all the boards are installed, tape over the butted seams with insulation tape.

Install siding or another protective layer over the insulation. Here, 2 × 4 ft. faux stone panels are being used. Once the panels are in place, backfill the trench with dirt or gravel. Make sure to maintain minimum slopes for runoff at grade.

Interior Wall Insulation

As a general rule, it is best to leave breathing space for the concrete or block so moisture that enters through the walls is not trapped. If your exterior basement walls meet the definition of a dry wall (see page 43) however, adding some interior insulation can increase the energy efficiency of your basement. If you are building a stud wall for hanging wallcovering materials, you can insulate between the studs with rigid foam—do not use fiberglass batts and do not install a vapor barrier. If you are building a stud wall, it's a good idea to keep the wall away from the basement wall so there is an air channel between the two.

Interior insulation can be installed if your foundation walls meet the conditions for dry walls (see page 43). It is important to keep the framed wall isolated from the basement wall with a seamless layer of rigid insulation board.

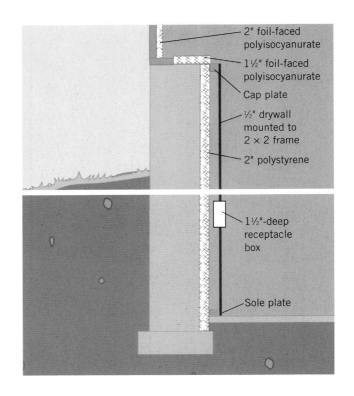

2" foil-faced polyisocyanurate
1½" foil-faced polyisocyanurate
Cap plate
½" drywall mounted to 2 × 2 frame
2" polystyrene
1½"-deep receptacle box
Sole plate

How to Insulate an Interior Basement Wall

Begin on the exterior wall by digging a trench and installing a 2"-thick rigid foam insulation board up to the bottom of the siding and down at least 6" below grade. The main purpose of this insulation is to inhibit convection and air transfer in the wall above grade.

Insulate the rim joist with strips of 2"-thick isocyanurate rigid insulation with foil facing. Be sure the insulation you purchase is rated for interior exposure (exterior products can produce bad vapors). Use adhesive to bond the insulation to the rim joist, and then caulk around all the edges with acoustic sealant.

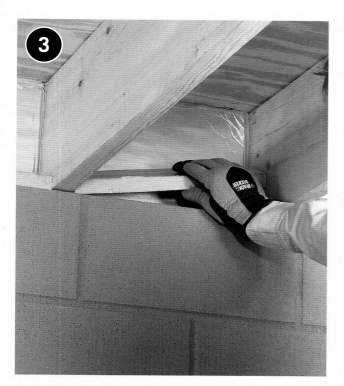

Seal and insulate the top of the foundation wall, if it is exposed, with strips of 1½"-thick, foil-faced isocyanurate insulation. Install the strips using the same type of adhesive and caulk you used for the rim joist insulation.

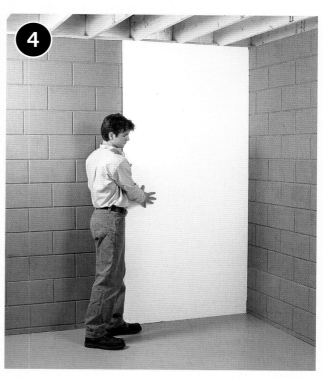

Attach sheets of 2"-thick extruded polystyrene insulation to the wall from the floor to the top of the wall with construction adhesive. Make sure to clean the wall thoroughly and let it dry completely before installing the insulation.

Seal the gaps between the insulation boards with insulation vapor barrier tape. Do not caulk gaps between the insulation boards and the floor.

Install a stud wall by fastening the cap plate to the ceiling joists and the sole plate to the floor. If you have space, allow an air channel between the studs and the insulation. Do not install a vapor barrier.

Improving Heating + Cooling

Finishing a basement or garage almost always requires that you expand your home heating system to heat the new space or add a supplementary heat source, such as electric baseboard heaters. Of these two options, installing baseboard heaters is an easier DIY project that won't compromise your existing heating. Installing a mini-split system can be a DIY project for an accomplished home handyperson, but most homeowners turn to a local company to install this sort of system.

Although the actual work may not be difficult, you should consult a heating and cooling professional before you decide to extend your furnace heat yourself. Home heating systems are delicately balanced, and making alterations may have ramifications throughout the system that result in your furnace becoming over-worked or other areas of your house being underserved. Remodeling can also create changes in your basement that impede the supply of fresh air to your furnace, so be sure to note the furnace location on your plans when you apply for a building permit.

Installing baseboard heaters is a good DIY solution for heating a basement room. They are inexpensive and relatively easy to install, and they will not impact your current home heating system.

A ductless mini-split system can be an relatively easy and inexpensive way to run heating and air conditioning to a basement. An exterior compressor is piped to an interior wall-mounted unit or units, and supplies climate control at the press of button.

Installing Baseboard Heaters

Baseboard heaters are a popular way to provide additional heating for an existing room or primary heat to a converted basement or garage.

Heaters are generally wired on a dedicated 240-volt circuit controlled by a thermostat. Several heaters can be wired in parallel and controlled by a single thermostat.

Baseboard heaters are generally surface mounted without boxes, so in a remodeling situation, you only need to run cables. Be sure to mark cable locations on the floor before installing drywall. Retrofit installations are also not difficult. You can remove existing baseboard and run new cable in the space behind.

TOOLS + MATERIALS

Drill/driver
Wire stripper
Cable ripper
Wallboard saw
Baseboard heater
  or heaters
Thermostat
  (in-heater or in-wall)

12/2 NM cable
Electrical tape
Basic wiring supplies
Flathead screws
Combination tool

HOW MUCH HEATER DO YOU NEED?

If you don't mind doing a little math, determining how many lineal feet of baseboard heater a room requires is not hard.

1. Measure the area of the room in sq ft. (length × width): _____

2. Divide the area by 10 to get the baseline minimum wattage: _____

3. Add 5% for each newer window or 10% for each older window: _____

4. Add 10% for each exterior wall in the room: _____

5. Add 10% for each exterior door: _____

6. Add 10% if the space below is not insulated: _____

7. Add 20% if the space above is not well insulated: _____

8. Add 10% if ceiling is more than 8 ft. high: _____

9. Total of the baseline wattage plus all additions: _____

10. Divide this number by 250 (the wattage produced per ft. of standard baseboard heater): _____

11. Round up to a whole number. This is the minimum number of feet of heater you need. _____

NOTE: It is much better to have more feet of heater than is required than fewer. Having more footage of heater does not consume more energy; it does allow the heaters to work more efficiently.

PLANNING TIPS FOR BASEBOARD HEATERS

- Baseboard heaters require a dedicated circuit. A 20-amp, 240-volt circuit of 12-gauge copper wire will power up to 16 ft. of heater.

- Do not install a heater beneath a wall receptacle. Cords hanging down from the receptacle are a fire hazard.

- Do not mount heaters directly on the floor. You should maintain at least 1 in. of clear space between the baseboard heater and the floor covering.

- Installing heaters directly beneath windows is a good practice.

- Locate wall thermostats on interior walls only, and do not install directly above a heat source.

How to Install a 240-volt Baseboard Heater

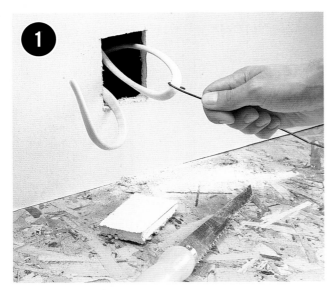

Cut a small hole in the drywall 3 to 4" above the floor at heater locations. Pull 12/2 NM cables through the first hole: one from the thermostat, the other to the next heater. Pull all the cables for subsequent heaters. Middle-of-run heaters will have two cables, while end-of-run heaters have only one cable.

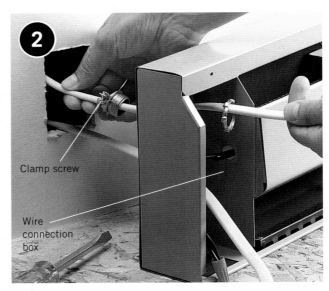

Clamp screw

Wire connection box

Remove the cover on the wire connection box. Open a knockout for each cable that will enter the box, then feed the cables through the cable clamps and into the wire connection box. Attach the clamps to the wire connection box and tighten the clamp screws until the cables are gripped firmly.

Anchor the heater against the wall about 1" off the floor by driving flathead screws through back of housing and into studs. Strip away the cable sheathing so at least ½" of sheathing extends into the heater. Strip ¾" of insulation from each wire using a combination tool.

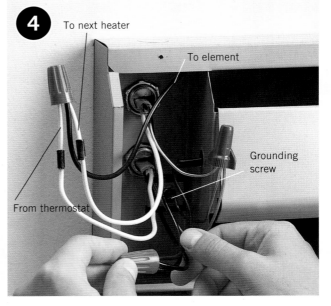

To next heater

To element

From thermostat

Grounding screw

Make connections to the heating element if the power wires are coming from a thermostat or another heater controlled by a thermostat. Connect the white circuit wires to one of the wire leads on the heater. Tag white wires with black tape to indicate they are hot. Connect the black circuit wires to the other wire lead. Connect a grounding pigtail to the green grounding screw in the box, then join all grounding wires with a wire connector. Reattach cover.

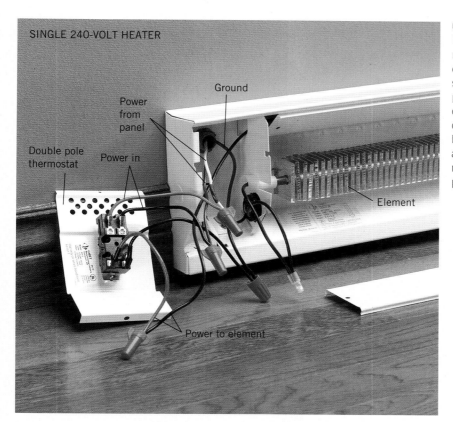

SINGLE 240-VOLT HEATER

Ground

Power from panel

Double pole thermostat

Power in

Power to element

Element

One heater with end-cap thermostat. Run both power leads (black plus tagged neutral) into the connection box at either end of the heater. If installing a single-pole thermostat, connect one power lead to one thermostat wire and connect the other thermostat wire to one of the heater leads. Connect the other hot wire to the other heater lead. If you are installing a double-pole thermostat, make connections with both legs of the power supply.

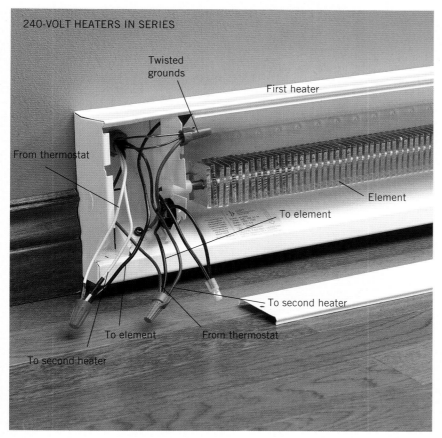

240-VOLT HEATERS IN SERIES

Twisted grounds

First heater

From thermostat

Element

To element

From thermostat

To element

To second heater

To second heater

Multiple heaters. At the first heater, join both hot wires from the thermostat to the wires leading to the second heater in line. Be sure to tag all white neutrals hot. Twist copper ground wires together and pigtail them to the grounding screw in the baseboard heater junction box. This parallel wiring configuration ensures that power flow will not be interrupted to the downstream heaters if an upstream heater fails.

Upgrading Ventilation

In basements it is especially important that air be kept moving constantly. High humidity levels combined with still or stagnant air leads to buildup of mold and mildew. If your basement rooms are part of a whole house, forced-air heating and cooling system, the natural air movement created when the system is operating will provide adequate air movement so no additional ventilation provisions need to be made (except in basement bathrooms, where a vent fan with an exterior exhaust is required).

If your basement has an independent heating system (such as electric baseboard heaters) and does not have air conditioning, add a ceiling-mounted vent fan in every room. If the rooms regularly have a musty odor, a vent fan is a good idea regardless of what type of heating and cooling plant you have.

Note: High-efficiency furnaces and water heaters have very specific requirements for fresh air intake supply. It is important that you consult with the furnace installer or your local plumbing inspector if you are making alterations to the airflow patterns in your basement.

WIRING A VENT FAN

This layout lets you place two switches controlled by the same 120-volt circuit in one double-gang electrical box. A single-feed cable provides power to both switches. A standard switch controls the light fixture and a time-delay switch controls the vent fan.

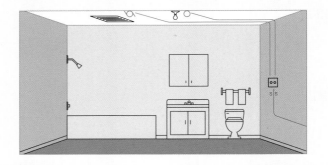

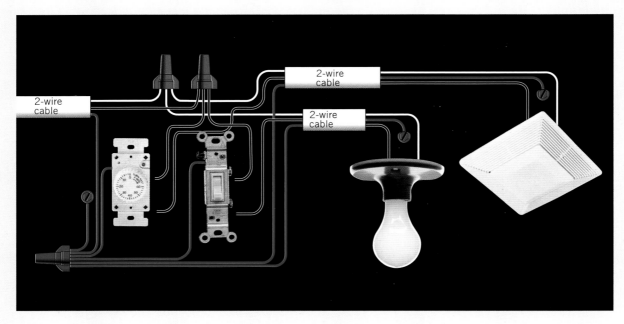

A vent fan is required in any basement bathroom. Hooking up the fan unit is easy, but running the exhaust ductwork can be tricky since it is normally vented outdoors through the rim joist.

Clothes dryers must be vented outdoors through ductwork. You may not vent them elsewhere in the basement.

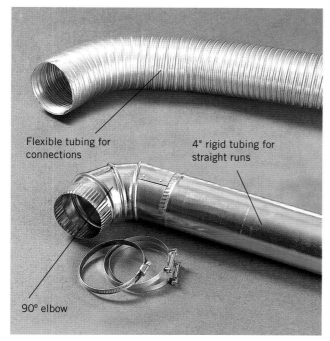

Flexible tubing for connections

4" rigid tubing for straight runs

90° elbow

Flexible metal tubing may be used to make the exhaust connection at the dryer, but the rest of the ductwork should be 4" rigid metal tubing.

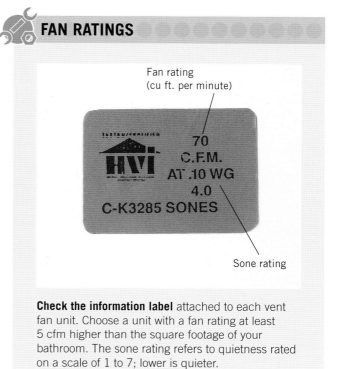

Fan rating (cu ft. per minute)

TESTED/CERTIFIED

HVI

70 C.F.M. AT .10 WG

4.0 C-K3285 SONES

Sone rating

Check the information label attached to each vent fan unit. Choose a unit with a fan rating at least 5 cfm higher than the square footage of your bathroom. The sone rating refers to quietness rated on a scale of 1 to 7; lower is quieter.

How to Install Ventilation Ducts

To plan your vent pipe route (it can be no longer than 25 ft. in most places), start outdoors by establishing the best location for the vent hood. The ideal location is concealed from sight and kept away from windows. In most cases, it is easiest to run the pipe through the rim joist of your house, but you may have to cut through a masonry foundation wall. Choose a spot and mark it with tape.

Look for a distinguishing point in the house structure that you can locate precisely on the interior side. A window, sillcock, or another penetration in the rim joist is perfect. Measure the distance from the point to the marked area where you want to install the vent hood.

On the interior side of the wall, generally in the basement, measure from the structural object you identified to see if the potential location for the rim joist entry is clear and accessible. Also check to see if you can make a relatively clean run to the vent fan, with minimal turns and minimal cutting of floor joists. Finding the best spot will probably take some trial and error and compromising.

Outline a hole that's slightly larger in diameter than the vent fitting that will go through the wall. Drill through the hole center into the rim joist using a bit that's long enough to penetrate the exterior. Drill until the bit breaks through into the light of day. *Note: Holes must be at least 2" from either edge of the joist and their diameter cannot be more than 1/3 of the joist width.*

Cut the siding using the drill hole in the siding as a centerpoint, draw the outline for the cutout on the siding of your house. Cut the hole out with a reciprocating saw and remodeler's blade.

Test the fit of the vent pipe assembly after you remove the cutout section of siding and joist material. Widen the hole if necessary. Once the assembly fits, slide the vent hood and pipe assembly into the hole so the vent hood flange fits as snugly against the siding as possible.

Attach the vent hood to the siding by driving screws at the corners.

Apply exterior-rated caulk around the perimeter of the vent hood to make a watertight seal. Snap on the protective cage, if provided, to keep small animals and vermin out.

Loosely pack fiberglass insulation between the vent duct and the edges of the opening you cut. Or, fill the gaps with minimal expanding spray foam insulation.

Run rigid metal ductwork from the vent hood to the fan. If you can, plan the route so you're installing the ductwork in the floor joist cavity. This will leave more headroom and lessen the chance of damaging the material.

Install an elbow at the end of the horizontal duct so it connects to the vent hood. Then add ductwork to connect the other side of the elbow to the vent.

Adding Electrical Circuits

Finishing a basement or garage almost always requires that you add electrical circuits to service the new space. To determine your electrical needs, think about the finished space and the types of fixtures you plan to include. Also, consult the local building department to make sure your plans comply with local codes. The following are some of the basic electrical elements to consider.

The National Electrical Code (NEC) requires receptacles to be spaced no more than 12 feet apart, but for convenience you can space them as close as 6 feet apart. You may need some non-standard receptacles, such as a GFCI (for bathrooms and wet areas), a 20-amp or 240-volt receptacle (for large appliances), and an isolated-ground receptacle (for a computer). Also consider the placement of furniture in the finished room; avoid placing receptacles or baseboard heaters where they may be blocked by furniture.

Lighting is an important consideration for every room, particularly rooms with limited sources of ambient light. Most codes require that each room have at least one switch-controlled light fixture, with the switch placed near the room's entrance. Stairways must have lighting that illuminates each step, and the fixture must be controlled by three-way switches at the top and bottom landings. Hallways and closets also need switch-controlled lights. In addition to meeting code requirements, your lighting plan should include different types of lighting to provide versatility for everyday tasks as well as visual warmth. This is especially true in basements, which generally need more artificial light than upper floors. It helps to use plenty of indirect lighting to eliminate shadows and provide ambient background light.

Your renovated space may need additional wiring to supply auxiliary HVAC equipment, such as a baseboard heater. If you'll be installing an electric radiant heating system for supplemental heat, find out what type of circuit wiring the system requires.

One way to avoid long wiring runs and crowding of the main service panel is to install a circuit breaker subpanel in or near the finished space. A subpanel gets its power supply from a single cable leading from the main panel. With adequate amperage, a subpanel can serve all of the circuits necessary for the finished space—all from a convenient location.

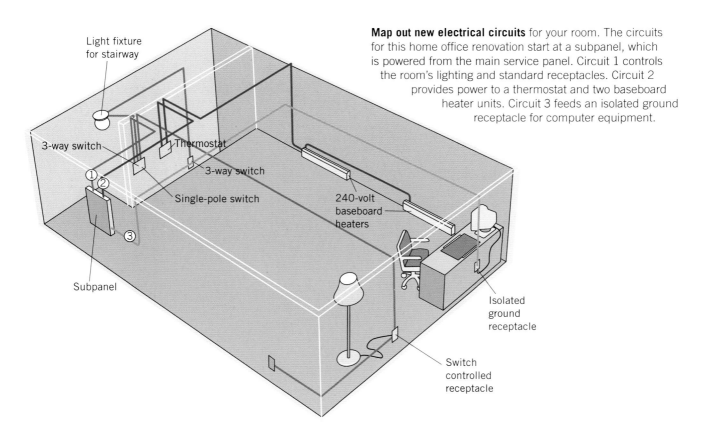

Map out new electrical circuits for your room. The circuits for this home office renovation start at a subpanel, which is powered from the main service panel. Circuit 1 controls the room's lighting and standard receptacles. Circuit 2 provides power to a thermostat and two baseboard heater units. Circuit 3 feeds an isolated ground receptacle for computer equipment.

Light fixture for stairway

3-way switch

Thermostat

3-way switch

Single-pole switch

240-volt baseboard heaters

Subpanel

Isolated ground receptacle

Switch controlled receptacle

Planning Wiring Circuits

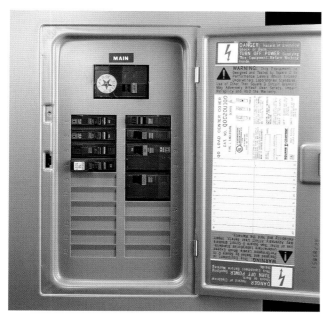

Examine your main service. The amp rating of the electrical service and the size of the circuit breaker panel will help you determine if a service upgrade is needed.

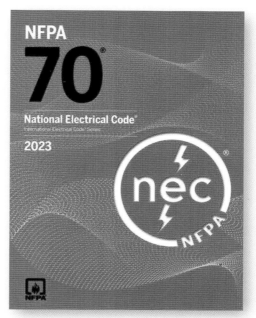

Learn about codes. The (NEC) and local electrical codes and building codes provide guidelines for determining how much power and how many circuits your home needs. Your local electrical inspector can tell you which regulations apply to your job.

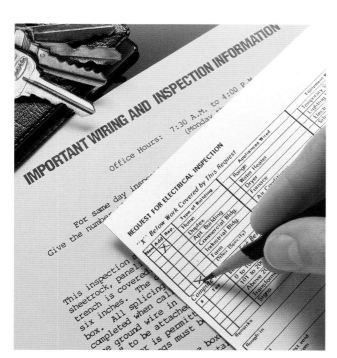

Prepare for inspections. Remember that your work must be reviewed by your local electrical inspector. When planning your wiring project, always follow the inspector's guidelines for quality workmanship.

Evaluate electrical loads. New circuits put an added load on your electrical service. Make sure that the total load of the existing wiring and the planned new circuits does not exceed the main service capacity.

Your Main Service Panel

Every home has a main service panel that distributes electrical current to the individual circuits. The main service panel is usually found in the basement, garage, or utility area, and can be identified by its metal box. Before making any repair to your electrical system, you must shut off power to the correct circuit at the main service panel. The service panel should be indexed so circuits can be identified easily.

Service panels vary in appearance, depending on the age of the system. Very old wiring may operate on 30-amp service that has only two circuits. New homes can have 200-amp service with 30 or more circuits. Find the size of the service by reading the amperage rating printed on the main fuse block or main circuit breaker.

Regardless of age, all service panels have fuses or circuit breakers that control each circuit and protect them from overloads. In general, older service panels use fuses, while newer service panels use circuit breakers.

In addition to the main service panel, your electrical system may have a subpanel that controls some of the circuits in the home. A subpanel has its own circuit breakers or fuses and is installed to control circuits that have been added to an existing wiring system.

The subpanel resembles the main service panel but is usually smaller. It may be located near the main panel, or it may be found near the areas served by the new circuits. Garages and basements that have been updated often have their own subpanels. If your home has a subpanel, make sure that its circuits are indexed correctly.

When handling fuses or circuit breakers, make sure the area around the service panel is dry. Never remove the protective cover on the service panel. After turning off a circuit to make electrical repairs, remember to always test the circuit for power before touching any wires.

The main service panel is the heart of your wiring system. As our demand for household energy has increased, the panels have also grown in capacity. Today, a 200-amp panel is considered the minimum for new construction.

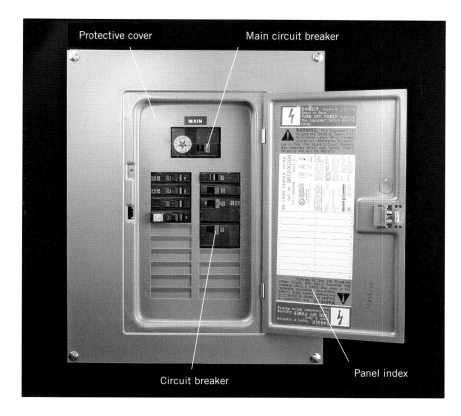

Protective cover   Main circuit breaker

Circuit breaker   Panel index

A circuit breaker panel providing 100 amps or more of power is common in wiring systems installed during the 1960s and later. A circuit breaker panel is housed in a gray metal cabinet that contains two rows of individual circuit breakers. The size of the service can be identified by reading the amperage rating of the main circuit breaker, which is located at the top or bottom of the main service panel.

A 100-amp service panel is now the minimum standard for all new housing. It is considered adequate for a medium-sized house with no more than three major electrical appliances. However, larger houses with more electrical appliances require a service panel that provides 150 amps or more; 200 amps are becoming the standard.

To shut off power to individual circuits in a circuit breaker panel, flip the lever on the appropriate circuit breaker to the OFF position. To shut off the power to the entire house, flip the main circuit breaker to the OFF position.

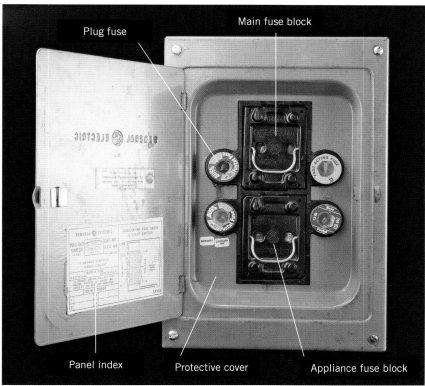

Plug fuse   Main fuse block

Panel index   Protective cover   Appliance fuse block

A 60-amp fuse panel is often found in wiring systems installed between 1950 and 1965. It is usually housed in a gray metal cabinet that contains four individual plug fuses, plus one or two pull-out fuse blocks that hold cartridge fuses. This type of panel is regarded as adequate for a small, 1,100-sq ft. house that has no more than one 240-volt appliance. Many homeowners update 60-amp service to 100 amps or more so that additional lighting and appliance circuits can be added to the system. Home loan programs also may require that 60-amp service be updated before a home can qualify for financing.

To shut off power to a circuit, carefully unscrew the plug fuse, touching only its insulated rim. To shut off power to the entire house, hold the handle of the main fuse block and pull sharply to remove it. Major appliance circuits are controlled with another cartridge fuse block. Shut off the appliance circuit by pulling out this fuse block.

Connecting Breakers for New Circuits

The last step in a wiring project is connecting circuits at the breaker panel. After this is done, the work is ready for the final inspection.

Circuits are connected at the main breaker panel if it has enough open slots, or at a circuit breaker subpanel. When working at a subpanel, make sure the feeder breaker at the main panel has been turned off, and test for power (photo, right) before touching any parts in the subpanel.

Make sure the circuit breaker amperage does not exceed the ampacity of the circuit wires you are connecting to it. Also be aware that circuit breaker styles and installation techniques vary according to manufacturer. Use breakers designed for your type of panel.

TOOLS + MATERIALS

Screwdriver
Hammer
Pencil
Combination tool
Cable ripper

Circuit tester
Pliers
Cable clamps
Single- and double-pole circuit breakers

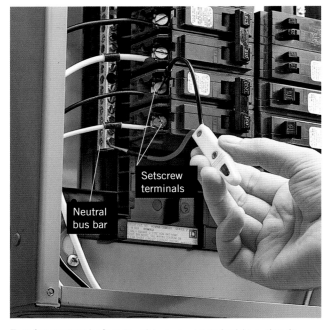

Test for current before touching any parts inside a circuit breaker panel. With the main breaker turned off but all other breakers turned on, touch one probe of a neon tester to the neutral bus bar, and touch the other probe to each setscrew on one of the double-pole breakers (not the main breaker). If tester does not light for either setscrew, it is safe to work in the panel.

How to Connect Circuit Breakers

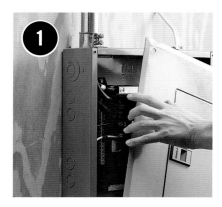

1

Remove the panel cover plate after you shut off the main circuit breaker in the main circuit breaker panel. (If you are working in a subpanel, shut off the feeder breaker in the main panel.) Take care not to touch the parts inside the panel. Test for power.

2

Open a knockout in the side of the circuit breaker panel using a screwdriver and hammer. Attach a cable clamp to the knockout.

3

Hold the cable across the front of the panel near the knockout, and mark the sheathing about ½" inside the edge of the panel. Strip the cable from marked line to end using a cable ripper. (There should be 18" to 24" of excess cable.) Insert the cable through the clamp and into the service panel, then tighten the clamp.

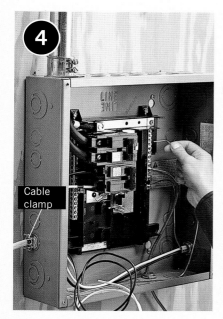

Bend the bare copper grounding wire around the inside edge of the panel to an open setscrew terminal on the grounding bus bar. Insert the wire into the opening on the bus bar, and tighten the setscrew. Fold excess wire around the inside edge of the panel.

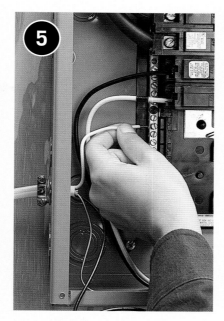

Bend the white circuit wire for 120-volt circuits around the outside of the panel to an open setscrew terminal on the neutral bus bar. Clip away excess wire, then strip ½" of insulation from the wire using a combination tool. Insert the wire into the terminal opening, and tighten the setscrew.

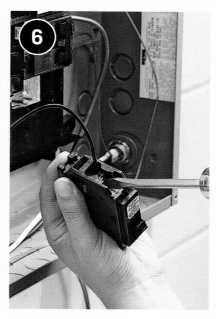

Strip ½" of insulation from the end of the black circuit wire. Insert the wire into the setscrew terminal on a new single-pole circuit breaker, and tighten the setscrew.

Slide one end of the circuit breaker onto the guide hook, then press it firmly against the bus bar until it snaps into place. (Breaker installation may vary depending on the manufacturer.) Fold excess black wire around the inside edge of the panel.

120/240-volt circuits (top): Connect red and black wires to a double-pole breaker. Connect white wire to the neutral bus bar, and grounding wire to the grounding bus bar. For 240-volt circuits (bottom), attach white and black wires to the double-pole breaker, tagging white wire with black tape. There is no neutral bus bar connection on this circuit.

Remove the appropriate breaker knockout on the panel cover plate to make room for the new circuit breaker. A single-pole breaker requires one knockout, while a double-pole breaker requires two knockouts. Reattach the cover plate, and label the new circuit on the panel index.

How to Run New Circuit Cable

Drill ⅝" holes in framing members for the cable runs. This is done easily with a right-angle drill, available at rental centers. Holes should be set back at least 1¼" from the front face of the framing members.

Where cables will turn corners, drill intersecting holes in adjoining faces of studs. Measure and cut all cables, allowing 2 ft. extra at ends entering the breaker panel and 1 ft. for ends entering the electrical box.

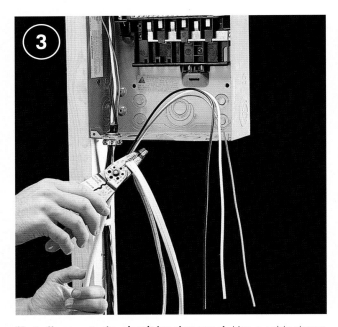

Shut off power to the circuit breaker panel. Use a cable ripper to strip cable, leaving at least ¼" of sheathing to enter the circuit breaker panel. Clip away the excess sheathing.

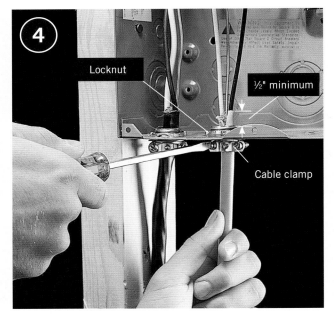

Locknut

½" minimum

Cable clamp

Open a knockout in the circuit breaker panel using a hammer and screwdriver. Insert a cable clamp into the knockout, and secure it with a locknut. Insert the cable through the clamp so that at least ½" of sheathing extends inside the circuit breaker panel. Tighten the mounting screws on the clamp so the cable is gripped securely, but not so tightly that the sheathing is crushed.

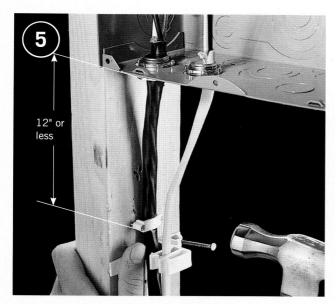

Anchor the cable to the center of a framing member within 12" of the circuit breaker panel using a cable staple. Stack-It® staples work well where two or more cables must be anchored to the same side of a stud. Run the cable to the first electrical box. Where the cable runs along the sides of framing members, anchor it with cable staples no more than 4 ft. apart.

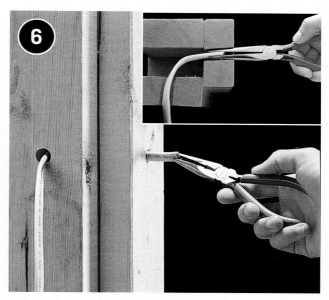

At corners, form a slight L-shaped bend in the end of the cable and insert it into one hole. Retrieve the cable through the other hole using needlenose pliers (inset).

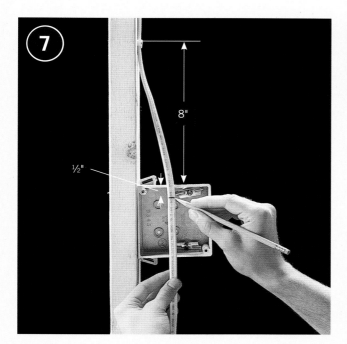

Staple the cable to a framing member 8" from the box. Hold the cable taut against the front of the box, and mark a point on the sheathing ½" past the box edge. Remove sheathing from the marked line to the end using a cable ripper, and clip away excess sheathing with a combination tool. Insert the cable through the knockout in the box.

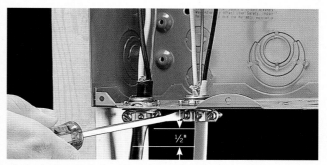

Variation: Different types of boxes have different clamping devices. Make sure cable sheathing extends ½" past the edge of the clamp to ensure that the cable is secure and that the wire won't be damaged by the edges of the clamp.

(continued)

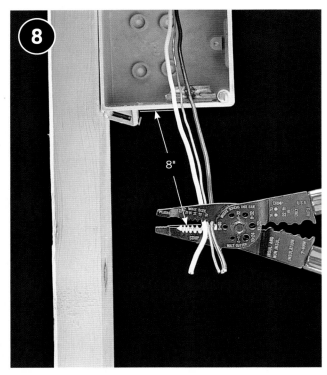

Clip back each wire as each cable is installed in a box, so that 8" of workable wire extends past the front edge of the box.

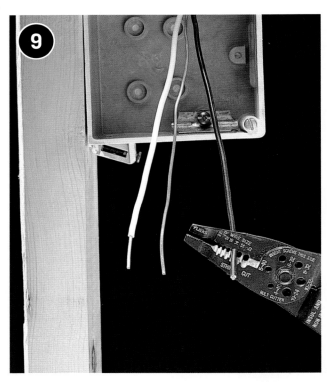

Strip ¾" of insulation from each circuit wire in the box using a combination tool. Take care not to nick the copper.

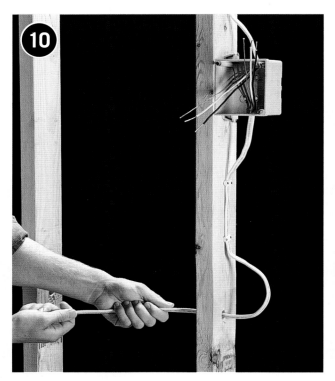

Continue the circuit by running cable between each pair of electrical boxes, leaving an extra 1 ft. of cable at each end.

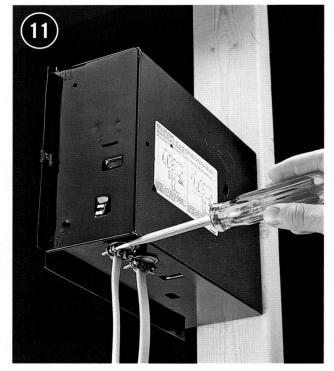

At metal boxes and recessed fixtures, open knockouts, and attach cables with cable clamps. From inside the fixture, strip away all but ¼" of sheathing. Clip back wires so there is 8" of workable length, then strip ¾" of insulation from each wire.

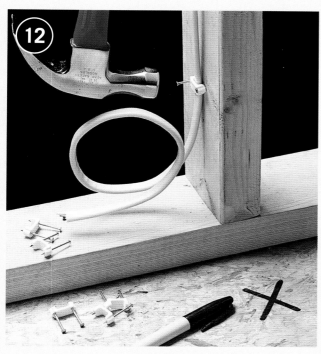

Staple the cable to a stud near the fixture location for a surface-mounted fixture like a baseboard heater or fluorescent light fixture. Leave plenty of excess cable. Mark the floor so the cable will be easy to find after the walls are finished.

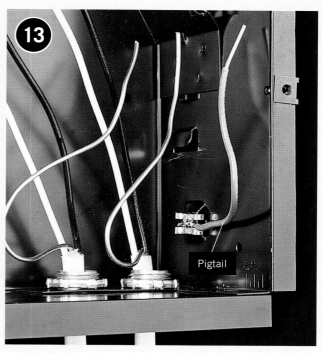

Pigtail

Connect one end of a grounding pigtail at each recessed fixture and metal electrical box, to the metal frame using a grounding clip attached to the frame (shown above) or a green grounding screw.

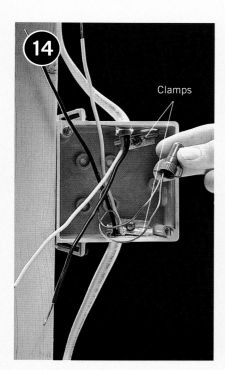

Clamps

Join grounding wires together with a wire connector at each electrical box and recessed fixture. If the box has internal clamps, tighten the clamps over the cables.

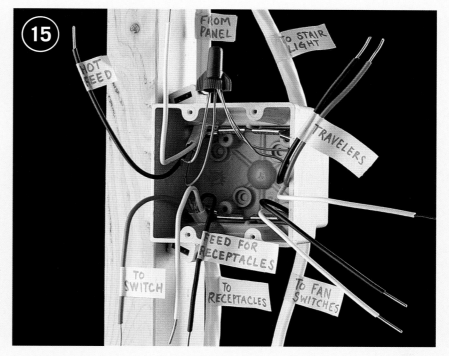

FROM PANEL

TO STAIR LIGHT

HOT FEED

TRAVELERS

FEED FOR RECEPTACLES

TO SWITCH

TO RECEPTACLES

TO FAN SWITCHES

Label the cables entering each box to indicate their destinations. In boxes with complex wiring configurations, also tag the individual wires to make final hookups easier. After all the cables are installed, your rough-in work is ready to be reviewed by the electrical inspector.

Garage Renovations

An underused garage is an amazing treasure. Garage conversions can be a money and energy-saving way to have a home addition without adding onto the actual structure of the house.

Most residential garages are just small enough to be manageable, but large enough to accommodate a full-scale, well-outfitted room such as a gym, home office, or home theater. The concerns of heating and cooling, ventilation, electrical, plumbing, and lighting are similar to what you would encounter in a basement conversion.

But, converting a garage to a livable space has its own unique considerations. To begin with, egress is less of an issue because most garages have at least two means of exit. Unlike in a basement, the integrity of the roof and the potential storage uses within the rafters are likely to play a part in any garage renovation.

This chapter covers some of the key and unique elements in converting this handy space. The projects outlined later in the book will apply equally to garages and basements.

In this chapter:
- Planning a Garage Conversion
- The Design
- The Garage Shell
- The Roof
- Garage-Specific Details
- Easy Storage Options

Planning a Garage Conversion

As with basements, any garage renovation should begin with a visit to your local building department. Local codes may dictate the extent to which you can alter or renovate your garage, and major changes will likely require permits and inspections.

An additional consideration that is unique to garages are lot-line issues. If your garage—attached or not—butts up to a property line, you'll want to consider your neighbors before settling on a use for the new room. This is especially true if you're planning on turning the garage into a band practice space or a spectacular home theater with surround sound for those action thrillers on your streaming list. Neighborhood or HOA noise rules won't necessarily stop you from transforming your garage into one of those spaces, but they will likely add planning and expense for sound-dampening insulation or wall and ceiling acoustic panels.

The initial stages of garage renovation planning involves a realistic appraisal of what you want to do with the structure. If you're willing to give up indoor space for your car, the garage can become just about any room you can imagine. It is ideal for a man cave or she shed, with a bar, pool table, ping pong table, comfortable seating, and fun décor. The isolated nature of the garage makes it ideal for self-contained socializing that won't impact the house proper (or disrupt individuals with earlier bedtimes).

At the very least, garages can be updated with customized storage that is both handsome and incredibly useful. Garages are also natural spots for fully equipped workshops that make woodworking, home DIY, or any other craft pursuit easier and more pleasurable.

SAMPLE GARAGE WORKSHOP FLOOR PLAN

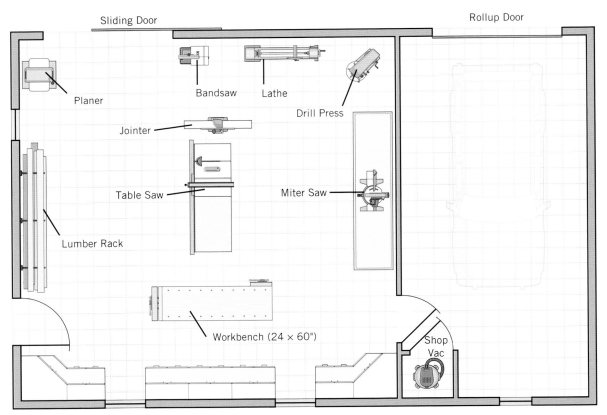

This floor plan represents one of the easiest, least expensive, and most common garage conversions, focused on a workshop. But a floor plan is a prerequisite no matter what the final space will be.

The Design

Once you've settled on the focus of your garage renovation, you'll begin the formal construction plan with a sketch or CAD floor plan. As with basement renovations, exact measurements are key. Usually, those are simpler with a garage, because the footprint is almost always a basic rectangle.

Those measurements will form the basis of your floor plan. The plan will ultimately have to take into account modifications to walls and ceiling. A garage renovation project offers much more flexibility than a basement renovation, even providing the potential to add doors and windows on at least three sides, as well as skylights above. These openings affect the use, so they should come before deciding where fixtures and other built-in elements will be placed.

Once you have an initial sketch and an idea of how you want to transform your garage, you'll have to consider the details that will make the structure livable and usable for whatever purpose you have in mind. The specifics include insulation (in colder areas, this may entail building out 2 × 4 stud walls to accommodate deeper layers of insulation), HVAC, and electrical upgrades similar to what you would consider for basement projects. But it may also entail changing the roof structure with, for instance, vented soffits to improve air circulation and natural cooling.

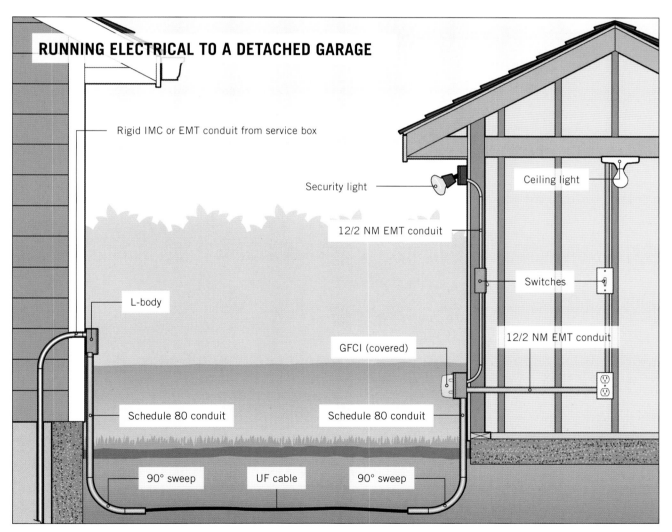

RUNNING ELECTRICAL TO A DETACHED GARAGE

Rigid IMC or EMT conduit from service box

Security light

Ceiling light

12/2 NM EMT conduit

L-body

Switches

GFCI (covered)

12/2 NM EMT conduit

Schedule 80 conduit

Schedule 80 conduit

90° sweep

UF cable

90° sweep

A basic outdoor circuit starts with a waterproof fitting at the house wall connected to a junction box inside. The underground circuit cable—rated UF (underground feeder)—runs in an 18"- to 24"-deep trench and is protected from exposure at both ends by metal or PVC conduit. Inside the garage, standard NM cable runs through metal conduit to protect it from damage (not necessary if you will be adding interior wall coverings). All receptacles and devices in the garage must be GFCI protected.

The Garage Shell

The actual shell of a garage highlights the key differences between upgrading a basement and renovating a garage. Where modifying concrete or masonry basement walls can be a mammoth task, the framed walls of a garage are much easier to alter. A garage also has space overhead that can be exploited for different purposes.

All that said, the shell must be in good condition before you begin finishing the interior. That means no rot, out-of-plumb walls, or other structural defects. Same goes for the roof; leaks or other flaws must be remedied before renovation.

Because most garage renovations ultimately involve outfitting the space with expensive tools, electronics, workout gear, or other pricey additions, a secure exterior door is essential. This means you may need to update your current access door if there is one, or it may involve adding one so that garage can be accessed without going through the house.

On the topic of doors, a garage renovation often entails removing the garage door and replacing it by framing in a wall. The basics of the framing process are outlined on page 122. Many older garages were framed with 2 × 4 studs rather the current standard of 2 × 6s. Match the new studs to the old to make the renovation as easy and seamless as possible.

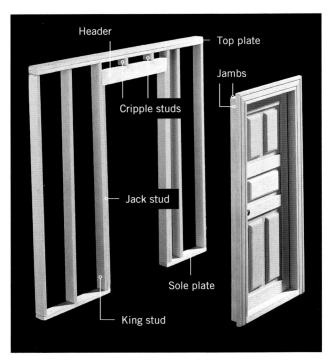

Door opening: The structural load above the door is carried by cripple studs that rest on a header. The ends of the header are supported by jack studs (also known as trimmer studs) and king studs that transfer the load to the sole plate and the foundation of the garage. The rough opening for a door should be 1" wider and ½" taller than the dimensions of the door unit, including the jambs. This extra space lets you adjust the door unit during installation.

The Roof

The overhead area is a key difference between basements and garages. The garage roof structure offers ventilation, light penetration, and storage opportunities.

For most homeowners, an "open chord" roof structure is obvious and easy storage potential. Simply laying a sheet of plywood across the lower chords (the joist between the two A-frame rafters) is a way to create ample semi-hidden storage.

But a garage roof offers even more for the DIYer who wants to put in a bit more expense and time. A skylight can amplify the light in the space for moderate cost and effort. Choose an operable model that open and closes to add ventilation.

ROOF TRUSSES OVERVIEW

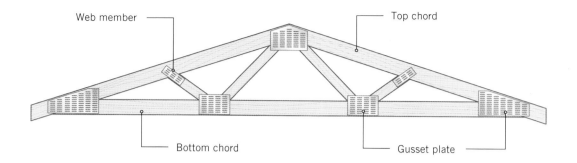

Web member — Top chord

Bottom chord — Gusset plate

Modern manufactured roof trusses are fabricated with upper and lower "chords," strengthened by web members fastened between the chords. This eliminates the possibility of truss storage. Older garages often have open trusses without the webbing. That creates the potential for overhead storage areas or vaulted ceilings.

A skylight can improve lighting and ventilation in a renovated garage space, and the installation process involves only modest DIY skills. The roofing is removed in the area and the hole cut in the roof sheathing. The skylight frame is then fastened in place, sealed with flashing tape, and new roofing felt and shingles are installed around the skylight.

Vinyl screened soffit strips, like the one shown here, are a wise choice for covering open soffits—or replacing solid soffits—during a garage renovation. These allow for ventilation while stopping bird and insect infiltration, and won't rot or degrade over time.

Garage-Specific Details

Much of what you'll need to do to convert a garage into your dream room is similar to what a basement conversion requires, and is well covered in other parts of this book. However, certain details are particular to the structure of a garage. For instance, the process of insulating the space is markedly different from how you insulate a basement.

Insulation is key to keeping the space comfortable throughout the seasons. Garages are traditionally insulated with faced fiberglass batts that have staple tabs, allowing them to be stapled into wall cavities between studs. However, a single layer of batts thin enough to fit into 2 × 4 wall cavities offers only modest insulation value. You can add layers, but that will require building out the wall with 2 × 2 furring strips screwed to the edges of the wall studs. This also creates the possibility of using more expensive rock wool batts (which will require installing hangers between studs to keep the batts in place). Rock wool not only provides a high insulation value, it is also a highly efficient sound dampener.

Creating an energy-efficient building envelope will require insulating the roof as well. This is a much easier process if you're drywalling a flat ceiling, because layers of unfaced fiberglass rolls can be laid across the ceiling joists. If you opt for vaulted ceilings, you'll have to settle for installing a thinner layer in the cavities between the rafters.

Insulating garage walls is simpler than working on basement surfaces. Fiberglass batts are stapled into wall cavities. If you live in an area with temperature extremes, it may well be worth your while to fur out the studs and add extra insulation.

Easy Storage Options

Garages lend themselves to accessible storage. Even if you're creating a space purely for entertainment purposes, like a home pub or theater, extra storage never goes to waste. The most basic option is pegboard mounted on the wall, which is a traditional favorite for garage workshops. Pegboards can also be adapted to function in a range of craft spaces.

Ceiling storage is of the most common in a garage, and there are many aftermarket systems for storage structures suspended from the ceiling.

However, for slightly more expense you can install a slat-wall system that allows you to customize storage for your precise needs. As a bonus, these systems tend to look bespoke, and can be integrated into most room designs.

A storage system like this one, with upscale, freestanding cabinetry framing an adjustable and customizable slat-wall storage system, is an eye-catching addition to any garage renovation.

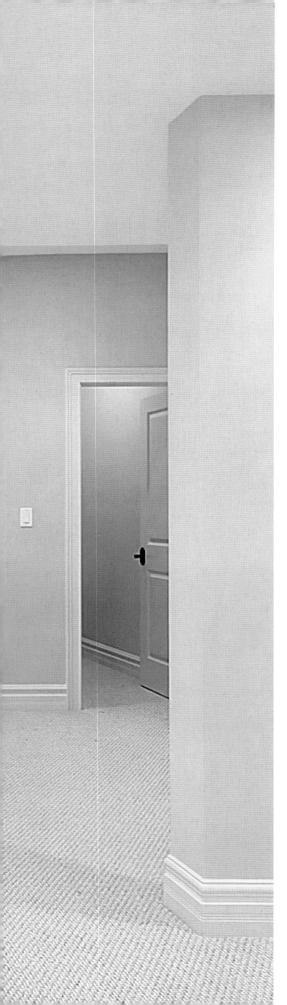

Basement Stairs

Unless you're rich enough to afford an elevator, your basement access will likely be via stairs. That means regardless of what you do with the square footage of the basement proper, you'll probably have to deal with building, upgrading, or at least sprucing up the staircase.

That process must focus on safety first. A rickety, creaky, compromised basement staircase should be remedied before you consider how you'll improve the look or style of those stairs—not to mention the space beyond.

Ensuring sound structural basics can entail improving the existing stair construction or replacing it altogether. The first questions to ask are, "Does the existing rise and run create comfortable access to the basement? Would the space be better served with a different staircase configuration (such as the introduction of a landing and an L turn)? Are the stairs wide enough?"

Only after you've answered those questions can you begin to address the issues of stairway style and decide between open or closed risers, wood or carpeted treads, and what type of handrail works best. Fortunately all those questions and more are answered in this section.

In this chapter:
- Stairway Types
- Renovating Stairs
- Adding a Stairlift

Stairways

Even though your basement most likely has an existing stairway, this essential element should still be part of your initial planning. Older basement staircases don't necessarily comply with modern building codes, and may need to be upgraded as part of your remodeling project. Making sure that the staircase meets or exceeds local building codes is only common sense; codes governing staircases were established based on time-tested realities about how people walk up and down stairs. Codes focus on safety and comfort, which should be your key concerns in any changes you make to your basement staircase.

Start with the basic measurements. Any staircase serving your basement should be as wide as possible, and comfortable to navigate. Otherwise, even the most beautiful basement rec room or home theater will be uninviting. Although you can build your own staircase (and you'll even find complete kits available that make the process fairly easy and straightforward), chances are that your basement already has a quite serviceable set of stairs. It's easy enough to adapt, upgrade, or renovate what's there, to specifically serve your remodeling goals.

Begin by fixing any obvious problems. Loose banisters or handrails, broken treads, risers or balusters, or even squeaky stairs, should all be remedied as part of a basement renovation. Small staircase problems can often turn into larger issues, especially when the traffic on the stairs increases.

But even if the existing structure is sound and in good shape, you may want to upgrade some parts of the staircase. A new railing with turned balusters and a detailed banister can bring a fresh new perspective—not only to the staircase, but to the entire basement. Changes like this will probably not challenge your DIY expertise, and can be hugely rewarding.

Bigger changes, including adding a landing, changing the direction of all or part of the staircase, or completely reinforcing the staircase, may call for some professional help. Because staircases are such essential access points, carefully consider the changes you want to make and how likely you are to complete them quickly and completely on your own. If you have doubts, best to call in a pro to help out.

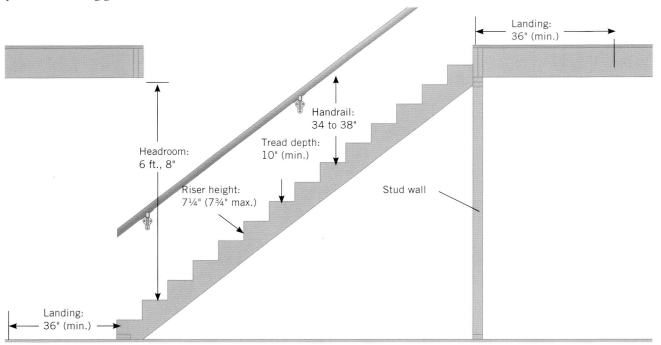

Basement stairs must be wide enough and within the allowable slope for rise and run. They also must have a grippable handrail and a clear landing area of at least 36 × 36" at both the top and bottom. They should be at least 36" wide with a minimum of 6 ft., 8" of headroom. If your house was built prior to the 1960s, there is a good chance the basement stairs don't conform to these standards (they may not even come close). Because you will be creating livable space, most municipalities will require that you upgrade or replace your stairs to meet the above requirements. Even if your local codes don't demand it, however, you should make upgrading your stairs phase one of your project anyway. Safety and convenience are reason enough.

Stairway Styles

L-Shaped Stair

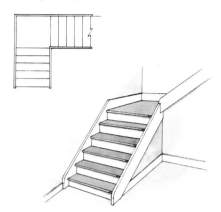

Straight Stair with Open Risers

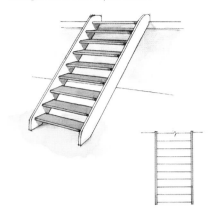

Standard Switchback Stair

Straight Stair

Switchback Stair with Winders

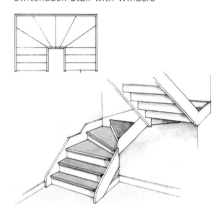

Switchback stair with Intermediate Flight

Side-flight Stair

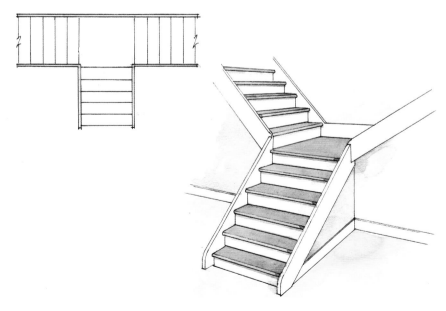

Depending on where they are located in a space, stairs can be freestanding (with no walls on either side) open on one side, or entirely enclosed by walls. As you will see, there are dozens of variations on these common types. *Note: Most building codes require staircase railings as a matter of safety; the staircases here are shown without railings for clarity.*

Renovating + Installing Stairs

If you're lucky enough to have a stable, structurally sound, and well-designed staircase leading to your basement, you may not need to do anything to improve access. Many basements, though, need some help in the stair department. Some staircases are too narrow to meet code for a bedroom or a home office (and likely are uncomfortable for multiple users). Other stairs have been exposed to moisture for so long that the wood may be compromised, rotten, or perhaps even infested with insects.

Often the quickest and simplest solution is to completely replace older, decrepit, and relatively unsafe stairs with a new staircase. The project here describes how to do that for a straight run of stairs without any intermediate landings. This choice was made for ease of illustration—to show readers the details in the clearest way possible. However, these type of prefab stairs come in a number of designs including, L-shaped, customizable curves, spirals, and more. They are sold as complete kits, with or without landings.

As with any project that involves user safety, the very first step in constructing new stairs for a basement is to consult with the local building or zoning department. Make sure whatever you build is not only up to code, but complies with best engineering standards and practices. It's essential to do this investigation prior to considering any prefabricated staircase kit to ensure it will comply with your local codes before you actually spend your money.

These kits normally include all the pieces and hardware you'll need to install the staircase. Most manufacturer's include a step calculator on the website or as a worksheet to determine how many steps you'll need for your particular staircase. Companies also offer guidance on installation, and variations to the straight-run model in this project, including dog-leg types, circular staircases, and U-turn versions.

Closed vs. Open

Most prefab staircases are "open" floating versions. This means that they don't have individual risers (the vertical piece that would stop your toe if you placed your foot too deep into the step) and don't include dual risers on either side; the stairs "float" on a central beam or post. This simplifies installation, creating a more open, airy, and modern look. However, some kits come with outside risers for a more traditional look and additional support.

If you prefer a more traditional, enclosed staircase, and need it built from scratch, it may be wiser to hire a carpenter with experience building stairs. Lastly, even in circumstances where codes may not require a handrail, it's always smart to include one. Make sure the kit you're buying comes with a handrail, because some do not.

TOOLS + MATERIALS

Tape measure	Phillips head screwdriver
Step ladder	Allen wrench set
Drill and bits	Cable cutters or hacksaw
Carpenter's pencil	4" lag screws
Torpedo level	
Box wrench set or socket wrench set	

How to Install Prefab Floating Basement Stairs

1

Measure the drop from the mounting platform to ensure you have enough steps for the recommended rise and run. Use the manufacturer's ordering calculator to determine the treads and posts you'll need. Check the kit after purchasing to ensure it contains all components on the part list. Stage them on a tarp or sheet in a clean, large work area as close as possible to the installation site.

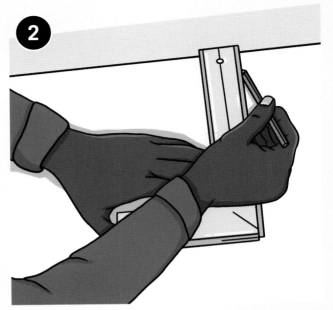

2

Measure and mark placement of the top, header bracket for the staircase. Measure out from the sidewall, then use a speed square to mark the bracket centerline. Be precise; use a stair tread to check that the bracket will be the correct distance from the wall.

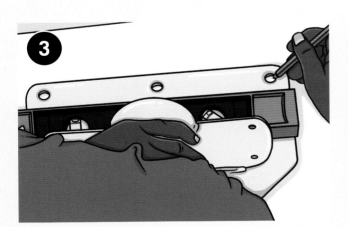

3

Hold the bracket in place. Using a torpedo level to ensure that the bracket is straight, mark the screw holes. Drill guide holes and then screw the top bracket to the upper platform ledger with 3" lag screws driven into anchors if they are not being screwed into framing members, or use the fasteners specified by the staircase manufacturer.

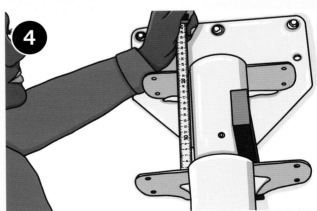

4

Install the bracket tube set screws, leaving them loose. Slip the second riser assembly's post up into the bracket tube. Measure and adjust the assembly's position for the correct rise. Make sure it's level both ways. Tighten the set screws slightly and check the distance from the tread platform to the wall; this should match the manufacturer's specifications (they usually call for a ⅛" to ¼" gap between the treads inside edge and the wall). Fully tighten the set screws.

5

Support the tread riser assembly with a 2 × 4 brace. Continue fastening subsequent tread riser assemblies, following the same process to ensure uniform rise, level, and distance from the wall.

6

Slip the platform base post into the final riser assembly and dry fit it to determine correct height from the final riser assembly to the base as it rests on the floor. Tighten the set screws. Drill guide holes in the floor for the base lag screws (this may entail using a masonry bit if you're screwing into a concrete slab). Screw the base to the floor.

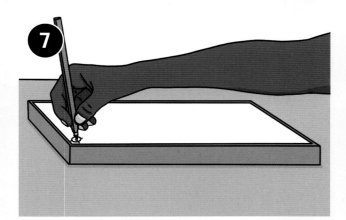

7

Remove the 2 × 4 brace. Use the manufacturer's supplied template (a template isn't supplied with all kits; use the manufacturer's measurements if not) to mark the handrail post holes in each tread. Drill all the holes at the same time.

8

Position the first tread on the top platform bracket and double check proper orientation (the handrail hole must be opposite the wall and to the back of the tread). Check level and drill pilot holes through the underside of the bracket into the tread bottom. Screw the tread in place with the supplied screws. Repeat with the rest of the treads.

(continued)

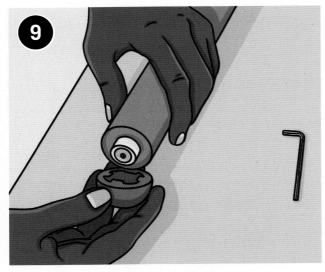

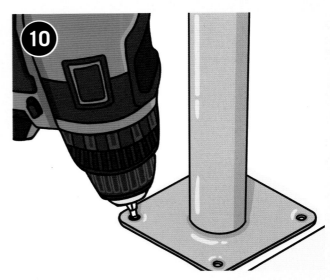

Prepare the handrails. For the kit shown here, pilot holes are drilled on each end of each wood handrail section. Screw a flange to both ends. Set-screw a cap to the flanges on one end of the two end handrail sections.

Measure and mark the placement of the top landing handrail support post bracket. Drill pilot holes and screw the bracket to the landing using 4" lag screws or screws and anchors, following the manufacturer's directions.

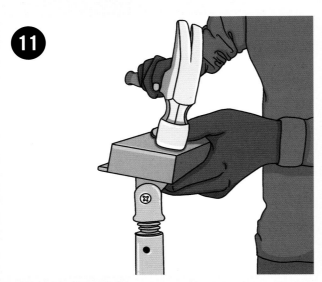

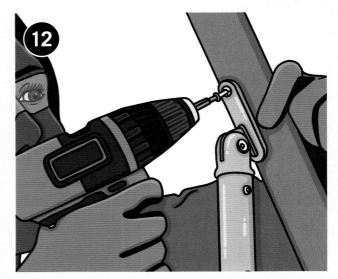

Fasten a handrail post to the first step through the predrilled hole, using the supplied bolt, washer, and nut. Check that the cable guide holes are facing the correct direction (parallel to the treads). Fasten the remaining handrail posts in the same way. Bolt a handrail mounting plate to each mount, and use a wood scrap block to tap the mount down into the top of each post. *Note: Handrail styles vary widely between staircase kits. This model includes metal posts and cables. Use the handrail construction supplied with your kit and follow the manufacturer's directions precisely to ensure user safety.*

Screw a hinged connector onto the open ends of each handrail section. Set the rail in place on the mounts correctly positioned, then screw it to the mounts from underneath. (A helper will make this process significantly easier.)

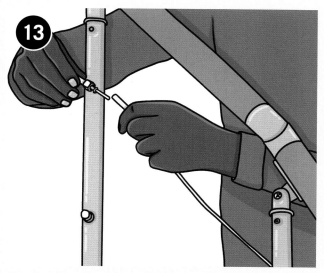

Slide the cable guides into the holes in the handrail posts. Thread the cable through the guides. At the top post, slip the end of the cable into the correct half of the tensioner, and tighten the setscrews onto the cable. Screw the two halves of the tensioner together through the cable guide.

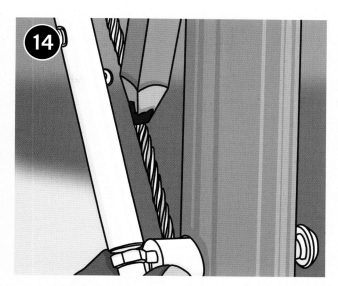

Pull the cable taut, measure and mark the bottom side of the cable for cutting. Cut the cable with cable cutters or a hacksaw, and secure it into the bottom tensioner in the same way you did at the top. Repeat with the remaining cables. Double check that all fasteners are completely tightened on the staircase and handrail.

REPAIRING EXISTING STAIRCASES

Sometimes all your basement staircase needs is a little TLC to make it workable for your new renovation. Repairing an existing staircase is easier and less expensive than replacing it, and requires little expertise. One of the most common issues—and irritations—with existing basement stairs is squeaking.

FIX SQUEAKS: FROM BELOW

Glue and screw small wood blocks to the seam between the tread and risers. As an alternative, coat the end of a wood shim with glue and tap it in between the risers, treads, and/or stringers. Use as many shims as it takes to stop the squeaking.

FIX SQUEAKS: FROM ABOVE

If the underside is inaccessible, you can drill pilot holes and screw down through the treads into the risers with small screws. Or nail a section of quarter-round molding to the riser and base along the seam where they meet.

Floors

In almost all cases, the starting point of your basement or garage floor will be a concrete slab. That humble stage forms the base for a vast number of potential flooring options. Choose any new flooring material for your basement renovation based on budget, comfort, and the look that appeals most to you.

You can simply put a new face on the concrete surface. Acid wash and stain the floor for an eye-catching mottled appearance, or lay down a coat of epoxy sealant for a more uniform look and incredible durability. Epoxy floor sealant comes in a number of colors and effects, including flaked. The main downside to treating the slab with a coating like epoxy, or just staining or painting it, is that the surface can be a bit hard and cold underfoot.

That's why many homeowners opt to cover the slab with entirely new flooring. With the concrete properly prepped, you can select from almost all of the options you would have over a wood subfloor. The one exception is carpet, which is used only where moisture is tightly controlled and there is no danger of water infiltration.

This section provides you with a guide through the various options. Depending on the size of the basement or garage, and the purposes for which you'll use the space, you may even mix and match flooring types. No matter what, you're sure to find an option that suits your circumstances and tastes.

In this chapter:
- Preparing Basement + Garage Floors
- Creating Decorative Concrete Finishes
- Installing Radiant Floors
- Laying Tile Floors
- Installing Laminate Plank Floors
- Laying Resilient Tile Floors
- Installing Rubber Roll Floors

Preparing Concrete Floors

Preparing a concrete floor for laminate, vinyl, or wood flooring has been simplified by the introduction of new subfloor products that have built-in vapor barriers and cleats that create a slight air gap between the subfloor and the concrete slab. This system allows air to circulate, protecting the finished flooring from any slab moisture. Dry-floor subfloor systems are less than one inch thick and are easy to install. The one most readily available and easiest to use is a product sold in 2 × 2 feet tongue-and-groove squares.

Although subfloor panels can be adjusted for slight irregularities in the concrete slab, they can't overcome problems with a floor that is badly cracked and heaved. Nor is the built-in air gap beneath the system a solution to a basement that has serious water problems. A badly heaved slab will need to be leveled with a cement-based leveling compound, and serious water problems will need to be rectified before you consider creating finished living space in a basement or garage.

Allow the subfloor panel squares to acclimate in the space for at least 24 hours with the plastic surfaces facing down before installing them. In humid summer months, the squares—as well as the finished wood flooring product, if that's what you'll be installing—should be allowed to acclimate for a full two weeks before installation.

The old way of installing subfloor (plywood over 2 × 4 sleepers) does make a sturdy floor and has the advantage of not requiring any special products—you can do it with materials found at any building center.

Instead of a subfloor and plywood underlayment, some flooring requires an isolation layer to separate it from the concrete basement floor. These are most often installed with ceramic floors.

If your concrete floor has cracks, holes, or other imperfections, address them before installing flooring.

Shown cutaway for clarity

Wood laminate flooring

Dry-floor sub-floor square

Underlayment

Basement slab

Concrete floors are functional, but whenever possible you'll want to cover them to improve livability in your new rooms. Some floor coverings can be installed directly over the concrete, but in most cases you should lay subfloor panels and underlayment before installing the floor covering. A system like the one above is ideal for basements because it can be removed readily: the laminate strip flooring snaps together and apart; the underlayment is unbonded and can be rolled up; and the subfloor panels also are snap-together for easy removal and re-laying.

APPLY FLOOR LEVELER

You can use mortar to level specific areas of a concrete floor as needed, or buy pourable, self-leveling versions to level a whole floor.

Leveling Concrete Floors

Level line

Laser level

Test the floor to see how level it is. Use a laser level to project a level line on all walls. Mark the line and then measure down to the floor. Compare measurements to determine if the floor is level. If you are installing a subfloor, you can correct the unevenness by shimming under low areas. But if the floor height varies by more than an inch, you should pour floor leveler compound in the low areas. In more extreme causes, you'll need to resurface the entire floor.

Break up and remove very high areas or eruptions, and patch the area with concrete that is leveled with the surrounding surfaces. Use a rental jack hammer to break up the concrete. A hand maul and cold chisel also may be used if the area is not too large: most concrete basement floors are only 3 to 4" thick.

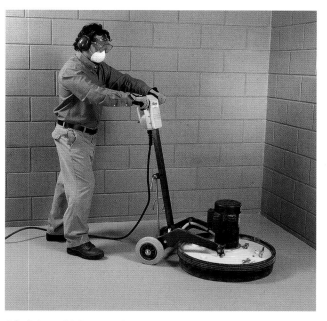

Grind down high spots if they are small and far apart. A rented concrete grinder makes quick work of the job. Even larger areas can be ground down, if your ceiling height is already limited (less than 7 ft.).

How to Repair Concrete Floor Cracks

Prepare the crack for the repair materials by knocking away any loose or deteriorating material and beveling the edges down and outward with a cold chisel. Sweep or vacuum the debris and thoroughly dampen the repair area. Do not allow any water to pool, however.

Mix the repair product to fill the crack according to the manufacturer's instructions. Here, a fast-setting cement repair product with acrylic fortifier is being used. Trowel the product into the crack, overfilling slightly. With the edge of the trowel, trim the excess material and feather it so it is smooth and the texture matches the surrounding surface.

How to Patch a Small Hole

Cut out around the damaged area with a masonry-grinding disc mounted on a portable drill (or use a hammer and stone chisel). The cuts should bevel about 15° away from the center of the damaged area. Chisel out any loose concrete within the repair area. Always wear gloves and eye protection.

Dampen the repair area with clean water and then fill it with vinyl concrete patcher. Pack the material in with a trowel, allowing it to crown slightly above the surrounding surface. Then feather the edges so the repair is smooth and flat. Protect the repair from foot traffic for at least one day and from vehicle traffic for three days.

How to Patch a Large Hole

Use a hammer and chisel or a heavy floor scraper to remove all material that is loose or shows any deterioration. Thoroughly clean the area with a hose and nozzle or a pressure washer.

OPTION: Make beveled cuts around the perimeter of the repair area with a circular saw and masonry-cutting blade. The bevels should slant down and away from the damage to create a "key" for the repair material.

Mix concrete patching compound according to the manufacturer's instructions, and then trowel it neatly into the damaged area, which should be dampened before the patching material is placed. Overfill the damaged area slightly.

Smooth and feather the repair with a steel trowel so it is even with the surrounding concrete surface. Finish the surface of the repair material to blend with the existing surface. For example, use a whisk broom to recreate a broomed finish. Protect the repair from foot traffic for at least one day and from vehicle traffic for three days.

Resurfacing a Concrete Floor

Badly degraded concrete floors can be restored by applying a topcoat of floor resurfacer. This cement-based product is designed to be poured on as a thick liquid so it can use gravity to find and fill in the low areas. After the resurfacer has set up, you will have a surface that's flat and smooth enough for installing just about any floor covering you choose, including padded carpet and floating floors with underlayment pads.

Concrete resurfacer typically should not be applied in layers thicker than one-half inch. If your floor has lower areas than this, fill them with sand-mix concrete first to get the low spots close to level, and then top with resurfacer over the whole floor.

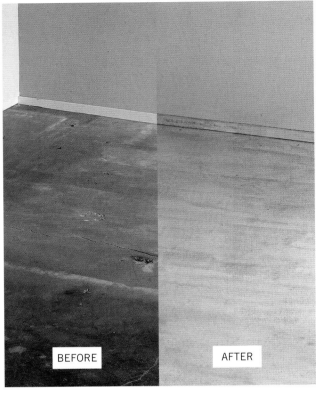

Concrete resurfacer offers an easy, inexpensive solution for renewing concrete surfaces in basements.

TOOLS + MATERIALS

Pressure washer	½" drill with paddle mixer
Steel concrete finishing trowel	Duct tape or backer rod
	Stiff-bristle brush
Long-handled squeegee	Concrete resurfacer
5-gallon bucket	

How to Resurface a Concrete Floor

Thoroughly clean the entire project area. If necessary, remove all oil and greasy or waxy residue using a concrete cleaner and scrub brush. Water beading on the surface indicates residue that could prevent proper adhesion with the resurfacer; clean these areas again as needed.

Wash the concrete with a pressure washer. Hold the fan-spray tip about 3" from the surface or as recommended by the washer manufacturer. Remove standing water.

Fill sizeable pits and spalled areas using a small batch of concrete resurfacer—mix about 5 pints of water per 40-lb. bag of resurfacer for a trowelable consistency. Repair cracks. Smooth the repairs level with the surrounding surface, and let them harden.

Section off the slab on a large project into areas no larger than 100 sq. ft. It's easiest to delineate sections along existing control joints. On all projects, cover or seal off all control joints with duct tape, foam backer rod, or weatherstripping to prevent resurfacer from spilling into the joints.

Mix the desired quantity of concrete resurfacer with water, following the mixing instructions. Work the mix with a ½" drill and a mixing paddle for 5 minutes to achieve a smooth, pourable consistency. If necessary, add water sparingly until the mix will pour easily and spread well with a squeegee.

Saturate the work area with water, then use a squeegee to remove any standing water. Pour the mix of concrete resurfacer onto the center of the repair area or first repair section.

Spread the resurfacer with the squeegee, using a scrubbing motion to make sure all depressions are filled. Then spread it into a smooth, consistent layer. If desired, broom the surface for a nonslip finish. You can also tool the slab edges with a concrete edger within 20 minutes of application. Let the resurfacer cure.

Creating Decorative Concrete Finishes

Most people are accustomed to thinking of concrete primarily as a utilitarian substance, but it can also mimic a variety of flooring types and be a colorful and beautiful addition to your renovated space.

Concrete is a hard and durable building material, but it is also porous—so it is susceptible to staining. Many stains can be removed with the proper cleaner, but sealing and painting prevents oil, grease, and other stains from penetrating the surface in the first place; and cleanup is a whole lot easier.

Even after degreasing a concrete floor, residual grease or oils can create serious adhesion problems for coatings of sealant or paint. To check to see whether your floor has been adequately cleaned, pour a glass of water on the concrete floor. If it is ready for sealing, the water will soak into the surface quickly and evenly. If the water beads, you may have to clean it again. Detergent used in combination with a steam cleaner can remove stubborn stains better than a cleaner alone.

There are four important reasons to seal your concrete floor: to protect the floor from dirt, oil, grease, chemicals, and stains; to dust-proof the surface; to protect the floor from abrasion and sunlight exposure; and to repel water and protect the floor from freeze-thaw damage.

TOOLS + MATERIALS

Acid-tolerant pump sprayer	Garden hose with nozzle
Alkaline-base neutralizer	Paint roller frame
Sealant	Paint
Rubber boots	Soft-woven roller cover
Rubber gloves	High-pressure washer
Roller tray	Paintbrush
Wet vacuum	Respirator
Acid-tolerant bucket	Stiff-bristle broom
Eye protection	Extension handle

Etching and sealing a concrete floor that is in good condition yields a slick-looking surface that has a contemporary feel and is easy to maintain.

How to Seal Concrete Basement Floors

Clean and prepare the surface by first sweeping up all debris. Next, remove all surface mud, wax, and grease. Finally, remove existing paints or coatings.

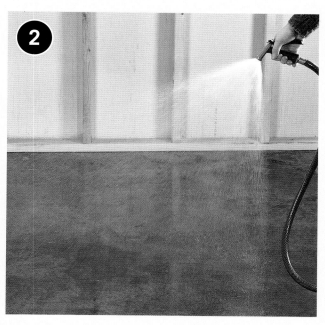

Saturate the surface with clean water. The surface needs to be wet before acid etching. Use this opportunity to check for any areas where water beads up. If water beads on the surface, contaminants still need to be cleaned off with a suitable cleaner or chemical stripper.

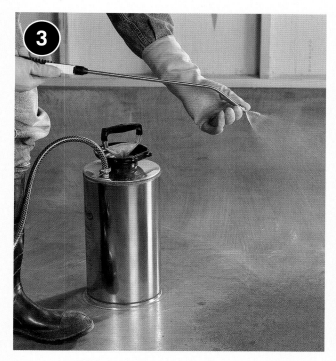

Test your acid-tolerant pump sprayer with water to make sure it releases a wide, even mist. Once you have the spray nozzle set, check the manufacturer's instructions for the etching solution and fill the pump sprayer (or sprinkling can) with the recommended amount of water.

Add the acid etching contents to the water in the acid-tolerant pump sprayer. Follow the directions (and mixing proportions) specified by the manufacturer. Use caution and wear safety equipment.

(continued)

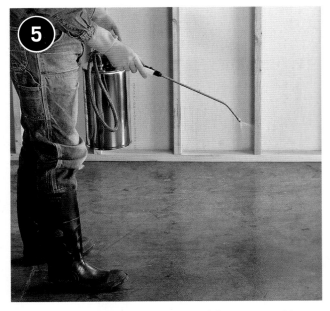

Apply the acid solution. Using the sprinkling can or acid-tolerant pump spray unit, evenly apply the diluted acid solution over the concrete floor. Do not allow the acid solution to dry at any time during the etching and cleaning process. Etch small areas at a time, 10 × 10 ft. or smaller. If there is a slope, begin on the low side of the slope and work upward.

Use a stiff-bristle broom or scrubber to work the acid solution into the concrete. Let the acid sit for 5 to 10 minutes, or as indicated by the manufacturer's directions. A mild foaming action indicates that the product is working. If no bubbling or fizzing occurs, it means there is still grease, oil, or a concrete treatment on the surface that is interfering. If this occurs, follow steps 7 to 12 and then clean the floor again.

Once the fizzing has stopped, the acid has finished reacting with the alkaline concrete surface and formed pH-neutral salts. Neutralize any remaining acid with an alkaline-base solution. Put 1 gal. of water in a 5-gal. bucket and then stir in an alkaline-base neutralizer. Using a stiff-bristle broom, make sure the concrete surface is completely covered with the solution. Continue to sweep until the fizzing stops.

Use a garden hose with a pressure nozzle or, ideally, a pressure washer in conjunction with a stiff-bristle broom to thoroughly rinse the concrete surface. Rinse the surface two to three times. Reapply the acid (repeat steps 5, 6, 7, and 8).

If you have any leftover acid, you can make it safe for your septic system by mixing more alkaline solution in the 5-gal. bucket and carefully pouring the acid from the spray unit into the bucket until all of the fizzing stops.

Use a wet/dry vacuum to clean up the mess. Some sitting acids and cleaning solutions can harm local vegetation, damage your drainage system, and are just plain environmentally unfriendly. Check your local disposal regulations for proper disposal of the neutralized spent acid.

To check for residue, rub a dark cloth over a small area of concrete. If any white residue appears, continue the rinsing process. Check for residue again.

Let the concrete dry for at least 24 hours and sweep up dust, dirt, and particles leftover from the acid etching process. Your concrete should now have the consistency of 120-grit sandpaper and be able to accept concrete sealants.

How to Stain a Concrete Floor

Thoroughly clean the entire floor. Use painter's tape and plastic sheeting to protect any areas that won't be stained, as well as surrounding walls and other surfaces. Test the spray of your garden sprayer using water: it should deliver a wide, even mist.

Dampen the floor with water using a garden sprayer. Mop up any pooled water, but make sure the entire floor is damp. Load sprayer with stain, and then apply the stain evenly in a circular motion until the concrete is saturated. Let the floor dry.

Remove the etching residue by soaking the floor with water and scrubbing vigorously with a stiff-bristled brush. As you work, clean up the liquid with a wet/dry vacuum. Dispose of the waste liquid safely, according to local regulations.

When the floor has dried completely (at least 18 to 24 hours), begin applying the sealer along the edges and in any hard-to-reach areas using a paintbrush.

Using a ⅜" nap roller, apply the sealer in 2 × 6-ft. sections, maintaining a wet edge to prevent lap marks. If the sealer rapidly absorbs into the concrete, apply a second coat after 2 hours. Let the floor dry for 18 to 24 hours before allowing light foot traffic and 72 hours before heavy use.

How to Paint a Concrete Floor

If you expect to use more than one container of paint, open them all and mix them together for a uniform color. You do not need to thin a paint for use on a floor. One exception is if you use a sprayer that requires thinned paint.

Using a nylon brush, such as a 2½" sash brush, cut in the sides and corners with primer. This creates a sharp, clean edge. Start this way for the topcoat as well.

Using a roller pad with the nap length recommended by the manufacturer, apply a primer coat to the surface. Start at the corner farthest away from the door, and back up as you work. Allow the primer to dry for at least 8 hours.

With a clean roller pad, apply the first topcoat. Make the topcoat even but not too thick, then let it dry for 24 hours. If you choose to add another topcoat, work the roller in another direction to cover any thin spots. Let the final coat dry another day before you walk on it.

Surfacing a Concrete Floor with Epoxy

Epoxy is an amazing material, even when it's used to coat and cover a basement or garage concrete floor. What started out as a durable and handsome concrete surface for institutional buildings and businesses has long become a favorite of homeowners looking to easily dress up any concrete floor.

The attraction lies in the variable appearance of an epoxied surface. Today's manufacturers offer "flakes" in a range of colors, and tints that can be used to create eye-catching custom appearances from solid colors to mottled and even water-like looks. In any case, a properly laid epoxy floor will be shiny and level, perfect as a stage for whatever you might have in mind for your basement or garage hideaway.

Easy to clean and hard to damage, quality epoxy products often come with 15-year warranties. Used on a basement or garage floor, the epoxy won't be exposed to the kind of abuse that might be expected in an industrial setting, meaning that the floor may easily last two decades or more in good condition. One of the main advantages over other flooring options, is that moisture—even flooding—won't damage the surface.

TOOLS + MATERIALS

Concrete grinder	5-gallon bucket
Work gloves	Squeegee
Paint respirator	9" lint-free woven roller
Safety glasses	with ⅜" nap
Safety earmuffs	Roller handle and
Tape measure	extension pole
Metal spike cleats	Spray bottle
Latex gloves	Isopropyl alcohol
Concrete floor epoxy kit	Denatured alcohol
Drill paddle attachment	

EPOXY BASICS

Given that the quality of your floor's appearance and longevity depends on the quality of the epoxy you use, this is not a place to cut corners in your basement renovation.

• Measure carefully and buy only the amount you need. You don't want to come up short but, unlike extra paint, there are few uses for leftover epoxy.

• Prep is key. The floor must be absolutely free from imperfections and contaminants such as grease. Rather than using powerful degreasers that could leave a residue and possibly ruin your floor's finish, clean the floor thoroughly with liquid clothes detergent and muriatic acid. If that doesn't do the trick and there are intractable oil stains, coat the floor with an oil-based primer meant for use under epoxy before laying down the epoxy.

• Be prepared for fumes and odor. You must use a respirator when laying an epoxy floor. Depending on the product you buy, it may off-gas powerful fumes. However, even if you can't smell the epoxy, it may be emitting unhealthy gasses. Ventilate the work area for 12 hours or more and wear a respirator.

• Opt for oil-based. Although water-based epoxies are easier to work with, they are less adhesive than oil-based products, and professionals consider them to be less durable.

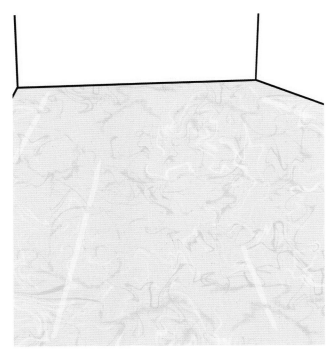

The range of colors and effects that can be achieved with tints, flakes, or other additives to a base epoxy are nearly unlimited. This is just one popular example—the appearance of water is achieved by randomly spreading a blue tint over the base and blending it in.

How to Epoxy a Concrete Floor

Assess the condition of the floor and prep it following the epoxy supplier's specifications. Remove all furniture or other obstructions. Sweep the space. Use a scraper to remove stuck-on material such as paint or carpet glue. Remove any oil or grease stains. Finally, use a grinder to create a uniform, rough surface that will bond completely with the epoxy. *Note: Concrete grinders can be rented at most large equipment rental stores.*

Use a wet/dry vac to suction up all dust on the floor. Damp mop the entire floor, changing the water frequently. Let the floor dry completely before proceeding. Tape off the base of any finished walls.

Mix the two parts of the epoxy base coat—adding metallics between the first and second part of the epoxy, if you're using them—following the supplier's directions. Use a 5-gallon bucket and a drill with a paddle attachment, and wear a respirator.

Immediately pour the base coat epoxy around the perimeter of the room, and then in rows across the floor. Use a squeegee to spread the epoxy in a relatively even layer. *Note: For larger floors this process will go much quicker and easier if a helper squeegees the floor behind the person pouring the epoxy.*

Cross-roll the surface after you have spread the epoxy with the squeegee. Even out the layer of epoxy.

Shake up the small bottle of highlight. Squeeze out small lines in a random pattern all over the floor. Use the squeegee to spread and blend the highlights. Hold the squeegee at a low angle and use it lightly to blend properly. You can use the roller to create a swirl effect.

Spritz the surface of the floor with isopropyl alcohol. After 10 minutes, apply a wider, more intense spray to the entire surface with denatured alcohol. Let the floor cure, undisturbed, for at least 12 hours at a temperature above 60°F and less than 90°F.

Installing Interlocking Floor Tiles

Interlocking floor tiles are another quick, DIY-friendly solution that can give your garage floor a custom checkerboard look. These 1 × 1-foot tiles are molded in a range of colors and are made of recycled PVC or other composites. You have several surface pattern styles to choose from, depending on the manufacturer. Some types are ventilated to promote drying, which makes them a good option for installing over damp concrete. The tiles will resist gasoline, oil, and most other solvents, so they're well suited for parking spaces or other garage workspace applications.

Interlocking tiles create a floating floor system similar to roll-out flooring. The four edges have locking tabs that clip together like a jigsaw puzzle. Once installed, the tile grid holds itself in place, so there's no need to fasten or glue the tiles permanently to the concrete. You can cut them with standard woodworking saws and tap them together with a mallet. Most tile brands offer beveled transition pieces to border the garage door edge.

The process for installing locking floor tiles is quite similar to laying permanent floor tile. Clean the floor thoroughly, then measure it and snap chalk lines to determine the exact center. Start by laying a row of

TOOLS + MATERIALS

Push broom or leaf blower	Straightedge guide
Tape measure	Rubber mallet
Chalk line	Jigsaw or circular saw
Stiff-bristle brush	Grease pencil
Cleaning detergent	Surface sealer
Backer board	Floor tiles
Plastic bucket	

tiles along the lengthwise chalk line from the garage door to the intersecting chalk line. Adjust the row as needed to allow for full tiles along the front edge of the garage. It's fine to have partial tiles along the back wall. Now, build out the tile grid left and right of the center row to fill in the rest of the floor. Measure and cut partial tiles as needed to fit against the side and back walls. Finish up by adding beveled transition pieces along the garage door, and cover the edges of the floor at the walls with sanitary base or other base moldings. With a helper, you should be able to complete your new tiled floor in an afternoon.

Interlocking floor tiles are easy to install because they just snap together, creating a durable floating garage floor that will hold up to wear and tear and even chemical spills. You can customize the look to suit your tastes. Given its long lifespan, this type of flooring is also inexpensive and a great value for money.

How to Install Interlocking Floor Tiles

Clean the floor by sweeping, vacuuming, or blowing off any debris with a leaf blower.

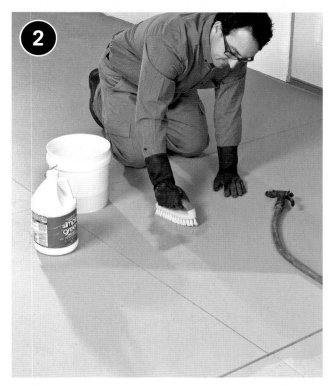

Remove any oily stains by scrubbing with detergent and a stiff-bristle brush.

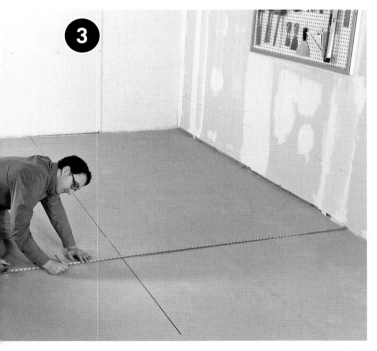

Measure the floor in both directions, and mark the locations of the centerlines.

Snap chalk lines to connect the center points in both directions, forming a point of intersection in the middle of the garage and dividing the floor into four quadrants.

(continued)

Lay tiles along one leg of the layout reference line, stopping just short of the wall. Snap the tiles together as you work. Use a rubber mallet to gently tap and set the tiles, if necessary.

Adjust the position of the first row of tiles so the last tile will fit just short of the overhead door opening without cutting. It is best to have the cut tiles against the far wall. If you plan to install a beveled transition strip (some, but not all, manufacturers carry them), be sure to allow room for it when repositioning the row. Snap new chalk lines parallel to the originals.

Add tiles along the adjusted reference lines to establish the layout. If you find that one row of tiles will need to terminate with tiles that are cut to a couple of inches or less, adjust the layout side to side so the cut tiles will be evenly balanced at both ends of the line. Fill in the tiles in the field area of all quadrants.

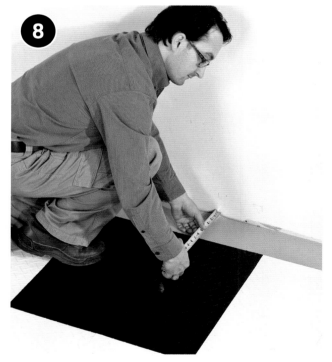

Measure the gaps at the ends of the rows requiring cut tiles and subtract ¼" for expansion.

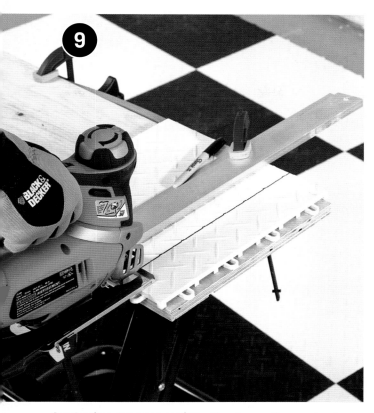

9

Cut the tiles that need cutting with a jigsaw. Be sure to place a backer board underneath the tile. Use a straightedge guide for a clean cut.

10

Install transition strips at doorways. Not all brands of interlocking tiles have transition strips available.

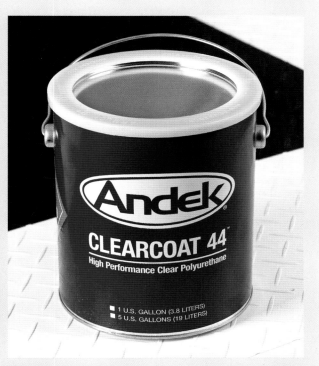

OPTION: Seal the tiles to protect against tire marks and other discoloration by applying a surface sealer. (Check with the tile manufacturer for its recommendations.)

11

Add base trim. Conceal the expansion gaps around the perimeter of the installation with molding, such as vinyl-cove base molding.

How to Install Subfloor Sleepers

THE SLEEPER SYSTEM

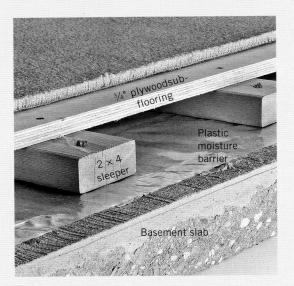

¾" plywood sub-flooring

Plastic moisture barrier

2 × 4 sleeper

Basement slab

Sleepers are strips of lumber (2 × 4 or 1 × 4) that are laid over a moisture barrier on a concrete floor to serve as nailers for the subfloor and to isolate it from direct contact with the concrete floor.

1

Roll out strips of 6-mil polyethylene sheeting. Overlap strips by 6", then seal the seams with vapor barrier, tape, or packing tape. Temporarily tape the edges along the walls. Be careful not to damage the sheeting.

2

Lay out pressure-treated 2 × 4s along the perimeter of the room. Position the boards ½" in from all walls (inset). *Note: Before laying out the sleepers, determine where the partition walls will go. If a wall will fall between parallel sleepers, add an extra sleeper to support the planned wall.*

3

Install sleepers using a circular saw, cut the sleepers to fit between the perimeter boards leaving a ¼" gap at each end. Position the first sleeper so its center is 16" from the outside edge of the perimeter board. Lay out the remaining sleepers using 16"-on-center spacing.

Where necessary, use tapered cedar shims to compensate for dips and variations in the floor. Place a 4-ft. level across neighboring sleepers. Apply construction adhesive to two wood shims. Slide the shims under the board from opposite sides until the board is level with adjacent sleepers.

Fasten the perimeter boards and sleepers to the floor using a powder-actuated nailer or masonry screws. Drive a fastener through the center of each board at 16" intervals. Fastener heads should not protrude above the board's surface. Place a fastener at each shim location, making sure the fastener penetrates both shims.

Establish a control line for the first row of plywood sheets by measuring 49" from the wall and marking the outside sleeper at each end of the room. Snap a chalk line across the sleepers at the marks. Run a ¼"-wide bead of adhesive along the first six sleepers, stopping just short of the control line.

Position the first sheet of ¾" plywood subfloor so the end is ½" away from the wall and the grooved edge is flush with the control line. Fasten the sheet to the sleepers using 2" wallboard screws. Drive a screw every 6" along the edges and every 8" in the field. Don't drive screws along the grooved edge until the next row of sheeting is in place.

Install the remaining sheets in the first row, maintaining an ⅛" gap between ends. Begin the second row with a half sheet (4 ft. long) so the end joints between rows are staggered. Fit the tongue of the half sheet into the groove of the adjoining sheet. If necessary, use a sledgehammer and wood block to help close the joint. After completing the second row, begin the third row with a full sheet. Alternate this pattern until the subfloor is complete.

Laying Rubber Tile

Rubber tile is a moisture-resistant, easy to install, and incredibly durable choice for the concrete floor of a basement or garage. Although the look isn't particularly upscale or to everyone's taste, rubber tiles are natural insulators against the chill of the concrete, forgiving of falls and bumps, and inexpensive. That's why they are typically used for home gyms, playrooms, workshops, or other rough-and-tumble spaces.

These tiles got their start in industrial buildings and garages, but manufacturers have since expanded their product lines to include a range of colors and patterns. Today's rubber tiles are a purely fun option for a basement where informality and play are the watchwords.

There is virtually no preparation for tile installation. You just need to make sure the concrete is clean, dry, and relatively level. The installation process itself—even for a large room—should take no more than an hour. However, as with all flooring, it's wise to leave the tiles in the room for at least 24 hours prior to installation, to acclimate them and account for expansion or contraction in the material.

TOOLS + MATERIALS

Rubber tiles	Chalk line
Tape measure	Utility knife
Sharpie	Work gloves
Framing square	

How to Install a Rubber Tile Floor

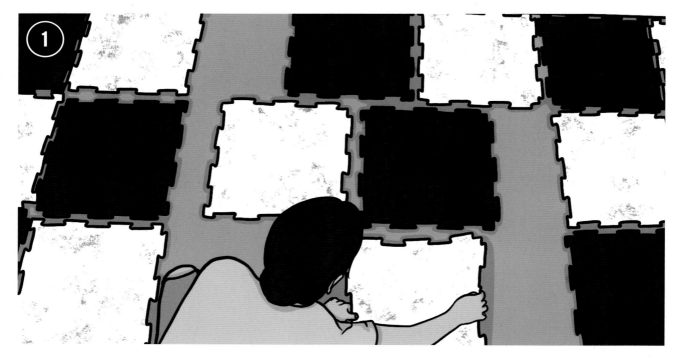

Double check the amount and type of rubber tiles are correct. Inspect for damage. Sweep and clean the concrete floor, making sure to remove any old adhesive. The floor should also be level. Set out the tiles, dry laying on the floor stacked in piles of two. Let them acclimate for 24 to 48 hours.

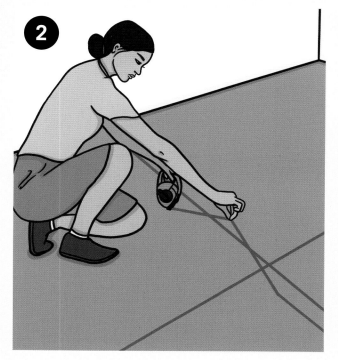

Snap perpendicular chalk lines crossing at the center point of the room.

Begin laying the tiles in perpendicular directions following the chalk line, to fill out one quadrant. The tiles may be fabricated with arrows marking the direction in which the tiles should be laid. Follow the manufacturer's instructions for the tiles you've bought.

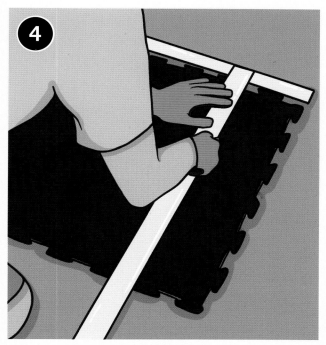

Lay all the field tiles, and then begin laying the edge tiles. Measure to the wall, accounting for a ¼" expansion gap. Transfer the measurement to the tile. Use a straightedge and a utility knife with a new blade to cut the tile, and then press it in place.

Once the floor is complete, check that all the tiles are securely pressed together. Sweep the floor, and then lightly damp mop. Allow the floor to dry before using.

Installing Laminate Plank Floors

Laminate flooring comes in a floating system that is simple to install, even if you have little experience. You may install a floating laminate floor right on top of plywood or a concrete slab, or over sheet vinyl or even hardwood flooring. Just be sure to follow the manufacturer's instructions.

The pieces are available in planks or squares in a variety of different sizes, colors, and faux finishes—including wood and ceramic. The part you see is really a photographic print. Tongue-and-groove edges lock pieces together, and the entire floor floats on the underlayment. At the end of this project there are a few extra steps to take if your flooring manufacturer recommends using glue on the joints.

The rich wood tones of beautiful laminate planks may cause you to imagine hours of long, hard installation work, but this is a DIY project that you can do in a single weekend. Buy the planks and all the materials and tools you'll need at a large home center or flooring store. Take careful measurements and follow the manufacturer's instructions closely, and you'll have a beautiful floor in no time without breaking a sweat.

TOOLS + MATERIALS

Drill	Foam insulation
Circular saw	Painter's tape
Hole saw	Chisel
Underlayment	Rubber mallet
½" spacers	Drawbar
Tapping block	Finish nails
Scrap foam	Nail set
Speed square	strap clamps
Manufacturer's glue	Threshold and screws
Adhesive tape	Utility knife

However, pay attention to the repetition of the floor pattern. Typically laminate floors include a limited set of surface prints, which will look unusual placed next to each other. That's why it's key to dry-lay the floor before final installation.

Laminate plank flooring can be the ideal solution for basement rooms. When installed as a floating floor over an underlayment pad, these planks go down quickly and are relatively inexpensive.

How to Install a Floating Laminate Floor

To install the underlayment, start in one corner and unroll the underlayment to the opposite wall. Cut the underlayment to fit using a utility knife or scissors. Overlap the second underlayment sheet according to the manufacturer's recommendations—usuallly about 4"—and secure the pieces in place with adhesive tape.

Working from the left corner of the room to the right, set ½" wall spacers and dry-lay planks (tongue side facing the wall) against the wall. The spacers allow for expansion. If you are flooring a room more than 26 ft. long or wide, you need to buy appropriate-sized expansion joints. *Note: Some manufacturers suggest facing the groove side to the wall.*

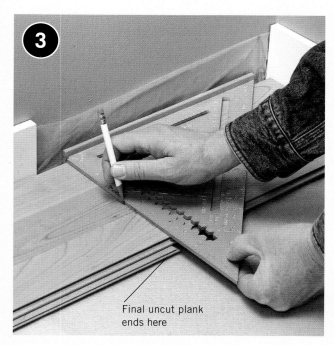

Final uncut plank ends here

Set a new plank right-side up on top of the previously laid plank, flush with the spacer against the wall at the end run. Line up a speed square with the bottom plank edge and trace a line. That's the cutline for the final plank in the row.

Press painter's tape along the cutline on the top of the plank to prevent chips when cutting. Score the line drawn in step 3 with a utility knife. Turn the plank over and extend the pencil line to the backside.

(continued)

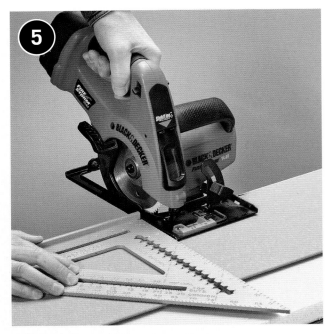

Clamp the board face down on rigid foam insulation or plywood to a work table. The foam reduces chipping. Clamp a speed square on top of the plank, as though you are going to draw another line parallel to the cutline—use this to eye your straight cut. Place the circular saw's blade on the waste side of the actual cutline.

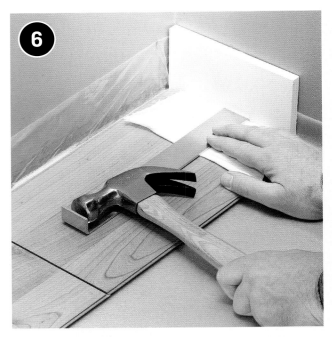

To create a tight fit for the last plank in the first row, place a spacer against the wall and wedge one end of a drawbar between it and the last plank. Tap the other end of the drawbar with a rubber mallet or hammer. Protect the laminate surface with a thin cloth.

Continue to lay rows of flooring, making sure the joints are staggered. This prevents the entire floor from relying on just a few joints, which keeps the planks from lifting. Staggering also stengthens the floor, because the joints are shorter and more evenly distributed.

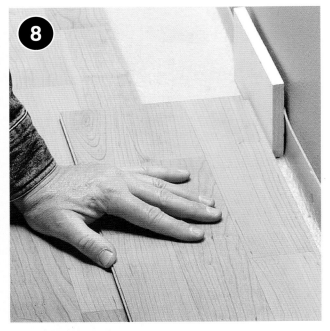

To fit the final row, place two planks on top of the last course; slide the top plank up against the wall spacer. Use the top plank to draw a cutline lengthwise on the middle plank. Cut the middle plank to size using the same method as in Step 3, just across the grain. The very last board must be cut lengthwise and widthwise to fit.

How to Work Around Obstacles

1

Marking outside
edge of the pipe

Mark indicates right
outside edge of the
pipe

Position a plank end against the spacers on the wall next to the obstacle. Use a pencil to make two marks along the length of the plank indicating the points where the obstacle begins and ends.

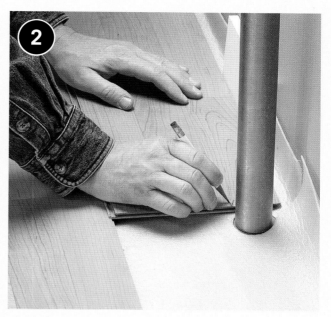

2

Once the plank is snapped into the previous row, position the plank end against the obstacle. Make two marks with a pencil, this time on the end of the plank to indicate where the obstacle falls along the width of the board.

3

Use a speed square to extend the four lines. The space at which they intersect is the part of the plank that needs to be removed to make room for the obstacle to go through it. Use a drill with a Forstner bit drill through the plank at the X You'll be left with a hole; extend the cut to the edges with a jigsaw.

4

Install the plank by locking the tongue-and-groove joints with the preceding board. Fit the end piece in behind the pipe or obstacle. Apply manufacturer-recommended glue to the cut edges, and press the end piece tightly against the adjacent plank. Wipe away excess glue with a damp cloth.

Installing Rubber Roll Floors

Once a mark of restaurants and retailers, sheet rubber flooring has become an option for homeowners as well. It's resilient, durable, and stable, holding up well under the heaviest and most demanding use. Better still, it's comfortable to walk on and easy to maintain.

The durability and resilience of rubber provide benefits in two ways. First, the flooring takes just about any kind of use without showing damage. Second, it absorbs shock in proportion to its thickness. Heavier rubber floors help prevent fatigue, making them comfortable for standing, walking, and even strenuous exercise.

Many new flooring products are made from recycled rubber, which saves landfill space and reduces the consumption of new raw materials. All this makes rubber flooring an environmentally friendly choice that will not affect indoor air quality.

To install rubber sheet flooring on top of wood, use only exterior-grade plywood, one side

sanded. Do not use lauan plywood, particleboard, chipboard, or hardboard. Make sure the surface is level, smooth, and securely fastened to the subfloor. It can also be installed right over clean, level concrete, using special adhesive.

TOOLS + MATERIALS

Adhesive	Mineral spirits
Chalk line	Notched trowel
Cleaning supplies	Painter's tape
Craft/utility knife	Straightedge
Flat-edged trowel	Weighted roller
Measuring tape	

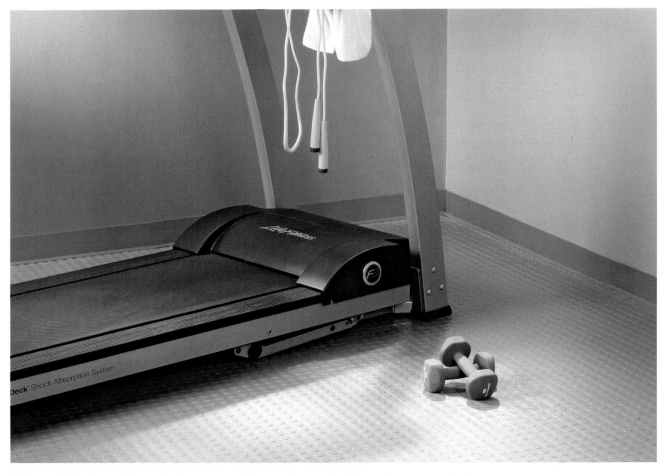

Rubber roll flooring resists water damage, provides cushion underfoot, and has a warm feeling.

How to Install Rubber Roll Flooring

Mark the first strip of rubber roll flooring for cutting to length. Start on the longest wall, and mark the cutting line so the strip will be a couple of inches too long. Use a straightedge guide to mark the cutting lines, and then cut with a sharp utility knife (be sure to put a backer board under the material before cutting it).

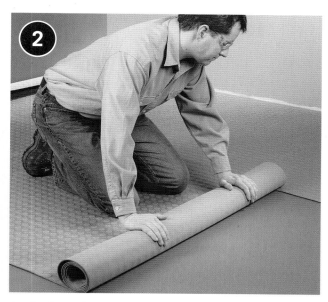

Set the first strip against the long wall so the overage in length is equal at each end. Cut the next strip to length and then butt it up against the first strip. Adjust the second strip so it overlaps the first strip by 1 to 1½", making sure the strips remain parallel. Lay out all of the strips in the room in this manner.

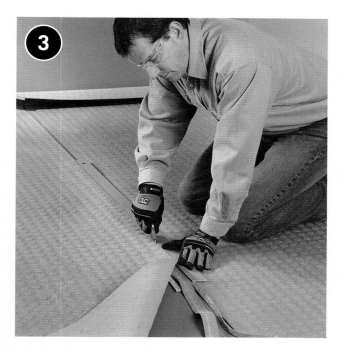

Cut the strips to create perfectly matched seams. With a backer board or concrete underneath the seam, center a straightedge on the top strip and carefully cut through both strips in the overlap area. Change utility knife blades frequently, and don't try to make the cut in one pass unless your flooring is very thin.

Remove the waste material from the seam area and test the fit of the strips. Because they were cut together, they should align perfectly. Make sure you don't adjust the position of one of the strips or the seams may not align properly.

(continued)

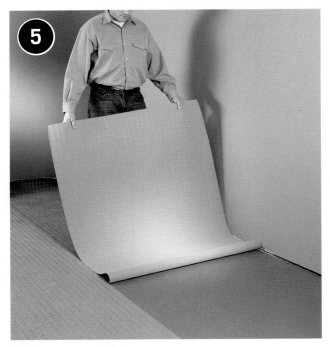

Fold back one half of the first strip so half of the flooring subbase is exposed. Again, take care not to shift the position of the flooring strip.

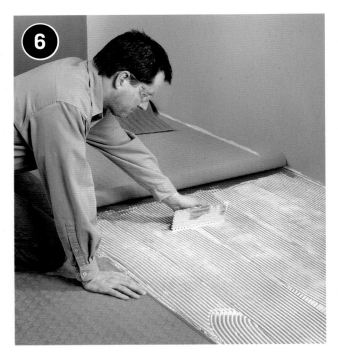

Apply the adhesive recommended by the flooring manufacturer to the exposed subfloor, using a notched trowel. Avoid getting adhesive on the surface of the rubber flooring, and make sure the adhesive is applied all the way up to the walls and just past the seam area.

Lower the roll slowly onto the adhesive, making sure not to allow any air to become trapped underneath. Never leave adhesive ridges or puddles; they will become visible on the surface.

Roll the floor immediately with a 100-pound roller to squeeze out any trapped air and maximize contact between the roll and the adhesive. With each pass of the roller, overlap the previous pass by half. Roll the width first, then the length, and re-roll after 30 minutes.

Fold back the second half of the first roll and the first half of the second roll. Apply and spread the adhesive as before. Spread the adhesive at a 90° angle to the seams. This will reduce the chance of having adhesive squeeze up through the seams. Continue installing strips in this manner.

Clean up adhesive squeezeout or spills immediately using a rag and mineral spirits. At seams, take care not to allow mineral spirits to get underneath the flooring, as it will ruin the adhesive.

Press down on any bubbles or on seams that do not have a seamless appearance. If a seam resists lying flat, set a board and weights over it overnight. It is a good idea to hand-roll all seams with a J-roller, in addition to rolling the entire floor with a floor roller.

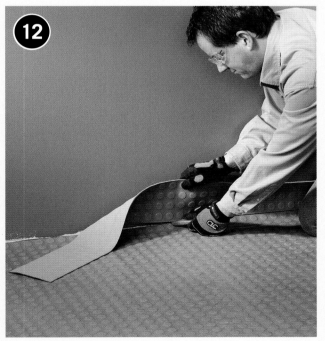

Trim off excess flooring at the ends using a utility knife. Leaving a slight gap between the flooring and the wall is fine as long as you plan to install base molding.

Walls + Ceilings

Choose from the same range of wall and ceiling surface options for your basement or garage as you would for any renovation in the home. However, some will be better than others, given the particular nature of the spaces—such as the high humidity in most basements. You may also need to make some special accommodations when installing basement or garage walls and ceilings, to accommodate the services essential to the rest of the house.

In basements it's wise to pay slightly more for special types of drywall or composite materials formulated to resist mold and moisture infiltration. Those are ideal choices for your dream subterranean space. The materials you use aside, keep in mind that these basic surfaces are regulated by the same codes that guide renovation in the home proper.

Once you've addressed those practical matters, you can dress up the space with special effects like tray ceilings (if you have the clearance), vaulted ceilings in a garage with open-chord trusses, wall moldings, and other decorative features. No matter what material is used to construct the walls and ceilings, you can also dramatically impact the look with paint color or other surface coverings.

In this chapter:

- Wall + Ceiling Options
- Framing Furred-Out Walls
- Building Partition Walls
- Framing Walls with Steel Studs
- Framing Soffits
- Installing Drywall
- Finishing Drywall
- Installing a Suspended Ceiling
- Installing an Acoustic Tile Ceiling

Wall + Ceiling Options

Framing walls, and finishing walls and ceilings, is done the same way in the basement as it is elsewhere in the house. However, it's a good idea to use pressure-treated lumber for sole plates that will rest on concrete. If you're covering your basement walls with drywall, choose a mold-resistant product. Some of these are paperless, eliminating the primary source of food for mold and mildew. Greenboard is standard drywall that has a moisture-resistant vinyl coating rather than paper, and is often used in shower and tub surrounds. Other types of drywall contain mold-inhibiting additives. Avoid moisture collecting finish surfaces such as wallpapers and paneling.

No matter how you clad your basement walls, you'll frame them in two basic ways. Walls built against masonry foundation walls are typically framed with furring strips. This type of wall can be tricky, and you should read the section on insulation (pages 122 to 123) for an important discussion on the intricacies of building against a foundation wall.

Partition walls divide large spaces, and are framed with standard construction grade 2 × 4s, or with metal studs. You can also frame walls along foundation walls in this manner (again, consult the section on insulation).

Ceilings are covered with drywall and, because moisture often isn't a problem in basement ceilings, standard drywall will usually suffice. Suspended and acoustic tile ceilings feature panels that—unlike drywall—can be easily removed to access electrical or plumbing lines in the joist cavities. However, these types of ceilings lower the height of the ceiling several inches. Look for ceiling panels that are mold resistant.

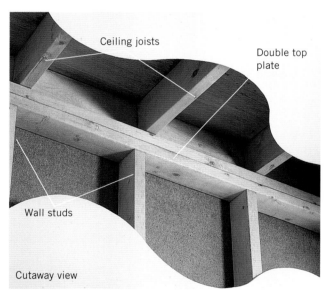

Load-bearing walls carry the structural weight of your home. In platform-framed houses, load-bearing walls can be identified by double top plates made from two layers of framing lumber. Load-bearing walls include all exterior walls and any interior walls that are aligned above support beams.

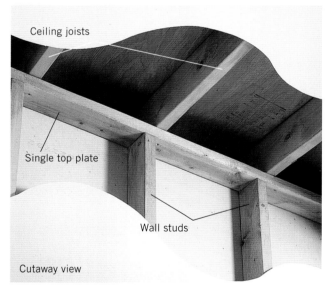

Nonloadbearing walls are interior walls that do not carry the structural weight of the house. They have a single top plate and can be perpendicular to the floor and ceiling joists but are not aligned above support beams. Any interior wall that is parallel to floor and ceiling joists is a partition wall.

Basement floors and walls are usually concrete, which can be hard surfaces to penetrate with traditional fasteners. The solution is a powder-actuated nail gun that uses a small charge of gunpowder to drive hardened nails into the concrete. These tools look and work like handguns. A steel barrel holds specially designed nails called *drive pins*. The nails have a plastic sleeve that keeps them centered in the barrel. The gunpowder charge is called the *powder load,* looks like a bullet, and fits into a magazine behind the barrel of the tool.

Squeezing the trigger—or hitting the end with a hammer (depending on the tool style)—fires the load, driving the pin at great force. Powder loads are made in a range of color-coded calibers to suit different applications and drive pin sizes. Follow the manufacturer's instructions carefully to choose the correct load for your task. These tools are easy to use and safe for indoor projects, provided you wear hearing and eye protection and follow all of the manufacturer's instructions.

Powder-actuated nail guns (PATs) are designed in two styles. Plunger types are activated by hitting the end of the shaft with a hammer, while trigger styles function like a handgun. With either type, the barrel must be depressed against the work surface to release a safety before a drive pin can be fired.

Powder loads contain various amounts of gunpowder inside a crimped shell. Color coding ensures that you're using the right amount of charge for your drive pin size and the materials you're fastening together. Follow the color charts carefully, starting with a low-powder charge.

How to Use a Trigger PAT

Be sure there's no powder load in the magazine, and prepare a PAT by sliding a drive pin into the barrel. Push it in until the tip is flush with the end of the barrel.

Slide the magazine open and insert a powder load into the barrel. A rim on the load shell ensures that it can only be loaded one way. Close the magazine.

Press the end of the barrel firmly against the work surface to release the safety. Squeeze the trigger to fire the drive pin. Once the pin is fired, slide open the magazine to eject the spent load shell.

Framing Furred-Out Walls

Wall framing members can be attached directly to a concrete foundation wall to provide a support for wall coverings and to house wires and pipes. Because they have no significant structural purpose, they are usually made with smaller stock called furring strips, which can be 2 × 2 or 2 × 3 wood. Do not install furring strips in conjunction with a vapor barrier or insulation, and do not attach them to walls that are not dry walls (see definition, page 43) with insulation on the exterior side. You can also fur out the edges of garage wall studs to increase wall cavity depth for deeper and more efficient insulation.

Furring strips serve primarily to create nailing surfaces for wallboard. Attach them to dry basement walls at the web locations of concrete block walls where possible.

How to Attach Furring Strips to Dry Foundation Walls

1

Cut a 2 × 2 top plate to span the length of the wall. Mark the furring-strip layout onto the bottom edge of the plate using 16"-on-center spacing. Attach the plate to the bottom of the joists with 2½" drywall screws. The back edge of the plate should line up with the front of the blocks.

2

If the joists run parallel to the wall, you'll need to install backers between the outer joist and the sill plate to provide support for ceiling wallboard. Make T-shaped backers from short 2 × 4s and 2 × 2s. Install each so the bottom face of the 2 × 4 is flush with the bottom edge of the joists. Attach the top plate to the foundation wall with its top edge flush with the top of the blocks.

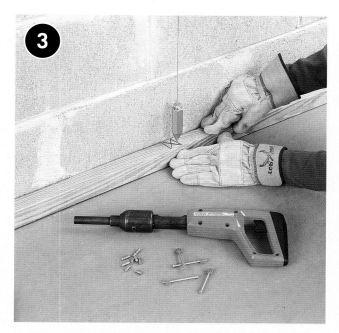

Install a bottom plate cut from pressure-treated 2 × 2 lumber so the plate spans the length of the wall. Apply construction adhesive to the back and bottom of the plate, then attach it to the floor with a PAT. Use a plumb bob to transfer the furring-strip layout marks from the top plate to the bottom plate.

Cut 2 × 2 furring strips to fit between the top and bottom plates. Apply construction adhesive to the back of each furring strip, and position it on the layout marks on the plates. Nail along the length of each strip at 16" intervals, using the PAT.

Option: Leave a channel for the installation of wires or supply pipes by installing pairs of vertically aligned furring strips with a 2" gap between each pair. *Note: Consult local codes to ensure proper installation of electrical or plumbing components.*

 ISOLATE THE WALL

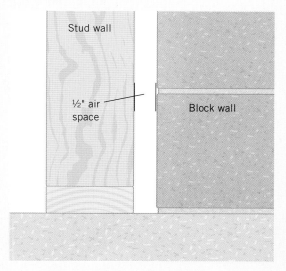

Stud wall

½" air space

Block wall

It consumes more floorspace, but a good alternative to a furred-out wall is to build a 2 × 4 stud wall parallel to the foundation wall, but ½" away from it. This eliminates any contact between the wall framing members and the foundation wall. See pages 124 to 126 for instructions on building a partition wall.

Building Partition Walls

Non-loadbearing, or partition, walls are typically built with 2 × 4 lumber and are supported by ceiling or floor joists above or by blocking between the joists. For walls that sit on bare concrete, use pressure-treated lumber for the bottom plates.

This project shows you how to build a wall in place, rather than how to build a complete wall on the floor and tilt it upright, as in new construction. The build-in-place method allows for variations in floor and ceiling levels and is generally much easier for remodeling projects.

If your wall will include a door or other opening, see pages 128 and 129 before laying out the wall. *Note: After your walls are framed and the mechanical rough-ins are completed, be sure to install metal protector plates where pipes and wires run through framing members.*

TOOLS + MATERIALS

Saw	Fiberglass sealant
Chalk line	2 × 4 lumber
Circular saw	Blocking lumber
Framing square	10d, 16d, and 8d
Plumb bob	common nails
Powder-actuated nailer	Concrete fasteners
T-bevel	Drywall screws
Tape measure	Acoustic sealant
Hammer	Masonry screws

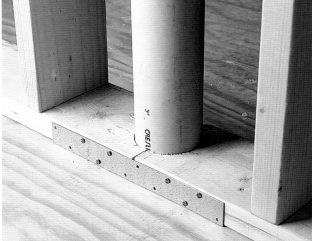

A typical partition wall consists of top and bottom plates and 2 × 4 studs spaced 16" on center top. Use 2 × 6 lumber for walls that will hold large plumbing pipes (bottom).

Variations for Fastening Top Plates to Joists

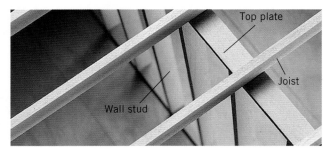

When a new wall is perpendicular to the ceiling or floor joists above, attach the top plate directly to the joists, using 16d nails.

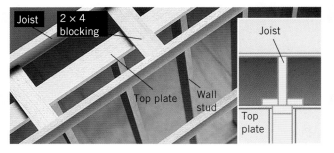

When a new wall falls between parallel joists, install 2 × 4 blocking between the joists every 24". If the new wall is aligned with a parallel joist, install blocks on both sides of the wall, and attach the top plate to the joist (inset).

How to Build a Partition Wall

Mark the location of the leading edge of the new wall's top plate, then snap a chalk line through the marks across the joists or blocks. Use a framing square or take measurements to make sure the line is perpendicular to any intersecting walls. Cut the top and bottom plates to length.

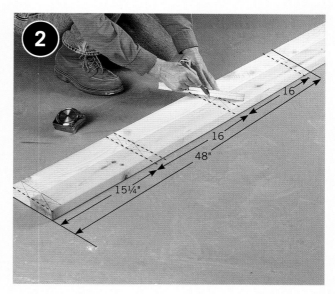

Set the plates together with their ends flush. Measure from the end of one plate, and make marks for the location of each stud. The first stud should fall 15¼" from the end; every stud thereafter should fall 16" on center. Thus, the first 4 × 8–ft. wallboard panel will cover the first stud and "break" in the center of the fourth stud. Use a square to extend the marks across both plates. Draw an X at each stud location.

Position the top plate against the joists, aligning its leading edge with the chalk line. Attach the plate with two 16d nails driven into each joist. Start at one end and adjust the plate as you go to keep the leading edge flush with the chalk line.

To position the bottom plate, hang a plumb bob from the side edge of the top plate so the point nearly touches the floor. When it hangs motionless, mark the point's location on the floor. Make plumb markings at each end of the top plate, then snap a chalk line between the marks. Position the bottom plate along the chalk line and use the plumb bob to align the stud markings between the two plates.

(continued)

Fasten the bottom plate to the floor. On concrete, use a powder-actuated nailer or masonry screws, driving a pin or screw every 16". On wood floors, use 16d nails driven into the joists or sleepers below.

Measure between the plates for the length of each stud. Cut each stud so it fits snugly in place but is not so tight that it bows the joists above. If you cut a stud too short, see if it will fit somewhere else down the wall.

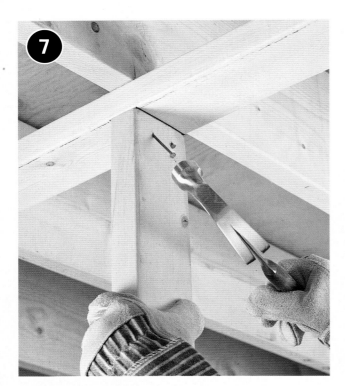

Install the studs by toenailing them at a 60° angle through the sides of the studs and into the plates. At each end, drive two 8d nails through one side of the stud and one more through the center on the other side.

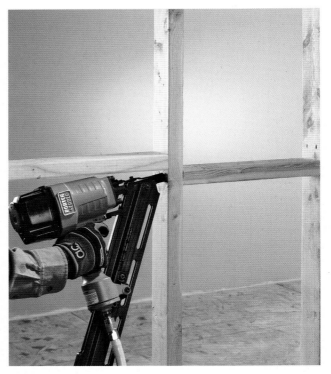

Option: If building codes in your area require fire blocking, install 2× cutoff scraps between the studs 4 ft. from the floor to serve this purpose. Stagger the blocks so you can endnail each piece.

Options for Framing Corners

L-corners: Nail 2 × 4 spacers (A) to the inside of the end stud. Nail an extra stud (B) to the spacers. The extra stud provides a surface to attach wallboard at the inside corner.

T-corner meets stud: Fasten 2 × 2 backers (A) to each side of the side-wall stud (B). The backers provide a nailing surface for wallboard.

T-corner between studs: Fasten a 1 × 6 backer (A) to the end stud (B) with wallboard screws. The backer provides a nailing surface for wallboard.

 ## How to Build a Soundproofed Partition Wall

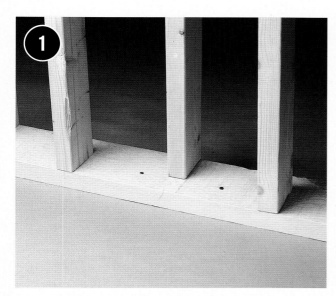

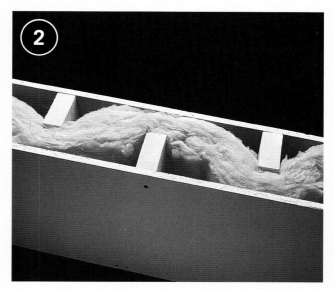

Frame new partition walls using 2 × 6 plates. Space 2 × 4 studs 12" apart, staggering them so alternate studs are aligned with opposite sides of the plates. Seal under and above the plates with acoustic sealant.

Weave R-11 unfaced specialty sound-blocking fiberglass blanket insulation horizontally between the studs. Cover each side with one or more layers of ⅝" mold-resistant specialty sound-blocking drywall.

How to Frame Door Openings

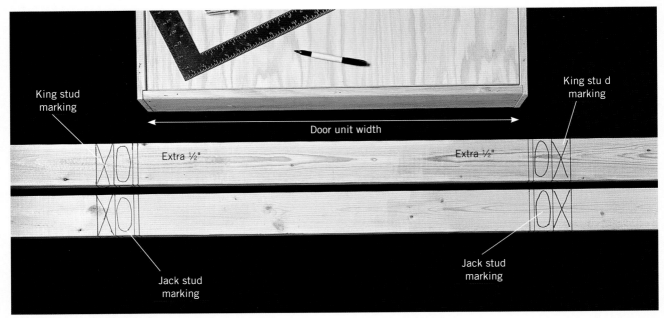

To mark the layout for the studs that make up the door frame, measure the width of the door unit along the bottom. Add 1" to this dimension to calculate the width of the rough opening (the distance between the jack studs). This gives you a ½" gap on each side for adjusting the door frame during installation. Mark the top and bottom plates for the jack and king studs.

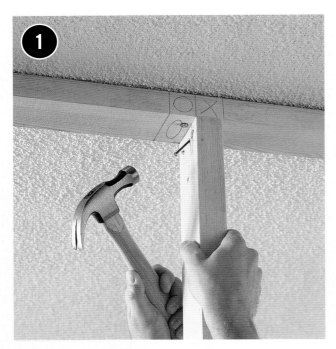

After you've installed the wall plates, cut the king studs and toenail them in place at the appropriate markings.

Measure the full length of the door unit, then add ½" to determine the height of the rough opening. Using that dimension, measure up from the floor and mark the king studs. Cut a 2 × 4 header to fit between the king studs. Position the header flat, with its bottom face at the marks, and secure it to the king studs with 16d nails.

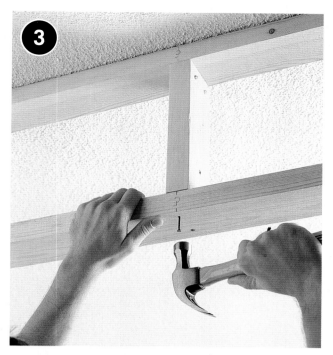

Cut and install a cripple stud above the header centered between the king studs. Install any additional cripples required to maintain the 16"-on-center layout of the standard studs in the rest of the wall.

Cut the jack studs to fit snugly under the header. Fasten them in place by nailing down through the header, then drive 10d nails through the faces of the jack studs and into the king studs

Option: Build a header from two pieces of 2 × 4 or 2 × 6, sandwiching a strip of ½" plywood. Structural headers are required in load-bearing walls, but it is very unlikely that you'll be creating new load-bearing walls in your basement. Still, if you are a fan of overbuilding, the header will create a sturdier wall.

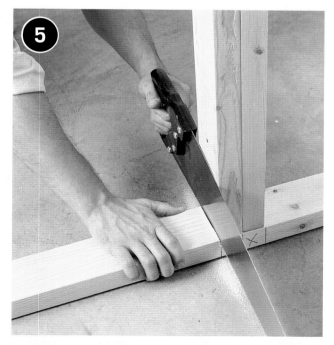

Saw through the bottom plate so it's flush with the inside faces of the jack studs. Remove the cut-out portion of the plate. *Note: If the wall will be finished with wallboard, hang the door after the wallboard is installed.*

Framing Walls with Steel Studs

Steel framing is quickly becoming a popular alternative to wood in residential construction due to the rising cost of wood and the advantages that steel offers. Steel framing is fireproof, insect proof, highly rot resistant, and lightweight. But the most significant advantage is that steel, unlike lumber, is always perfectly uniform and straight.

Steel studs and tracks (or plates) are commonly available at home centers and lumberyards in nominal widths comparable to their wooden counterparts: 1⅝" (2 × 2), 2½" (2 × 3), 3⅝" (2 × 4), and 5½" (2 × 6). Although 25-gauge (or 18-mil) and 20-gauge (or 33-mil) steel framing is suitable for most non-load-bearing partition walls and soffits that will be covered with wallboard, 20-gauge results in a somewhat sturdier wall. Use 20-gauge studs for walls that will receive cementboard.

With a few exceptions, the layout and framing methods used for a steel-frame partition wall are the same as those used for a wood-frame wall.

Here are a few tips for working with steel:

• Steel framing is fastened together with screws, not nails. Attach steel tracks to existing wood framing using long drywall screws.

• Even pressure and slow drill speed make it easy to start screws. Drive the screws down tight, but be careful not to strip the steel. Don't use drill-point screws with 25-gauge steel, which can strip easily.

• Most steel studs have punch-outs for running plumbing and electrical lines through the framing. Cut the studs to length from the same end to keep the punch-outs lined up.

• The hand-cut edges of steel framing are very sharp; wear heavy gloves when handling them.

• To provide support for electrical receptacle boxes, use boxes with special bracing for steel studs, or fasten boxes to wood framing installed between the studs.

• Use 16"-wide batts for insulating between steel studs. The added width allows for a friction fit, whereas standard batts would slide down.

Steel framing, when coupled with wallboard, creates a rigid wall system as solid and strong as wood-framed walls. Steel track is used to create plates, headers, and sills. Steel studs are installed so the open side faces in the same direction, except at door, window, or other openings. The punch-outs in studs are for running utility lines through the framing.

Steel studs and tracks have the same basic structure—a web that spans two flange sides—however, studs also contain a ¼" lip to improve their rigidity.

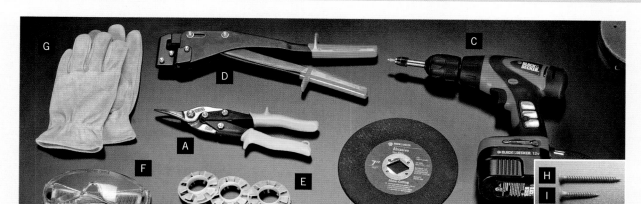

Steel framing requires a few specialty tools and materials. Aviation snips (A) are needed to cut tracks and studs, though a miter saw outfitted with a steel-cutting abrasive blade (B) can speed up the process. A drill or screwgun (C) is required for fastening framing. Handy for large projects, a stud crimper (D) creates mechanical joints between tracks and studs. Plastic grommets (E) are placed in punch-outs to help protected gas and power lines. Protective eyewear and heavy work gloves (F, G) are necessities when working with hand-cut steel framing. Use self-tapping screws (inset) to fasten steel components. To install wood trim, use Type S trim head screws (H); to fasten wallboard, Type S wallboard screws (I); and to fasten studs and tracks together, $\frac{7}{16}$" Type S panhead screws (J).

TIPS FOR FRAMING WITH STEEL

Fastening tab

When running metal plumbing pipe and electrical cable through steel studs, use plastic grommets at punch-outs to prevent galvanic action and electrification of the wall. Install wood blocking between studs for hanging decorative accessories or wainscoting.

Frame door openings 3" wider and 1½" taller than normal, then wrap the insides with 2 × 4s to provide a nailing surface for hanging the door and installing the casing.

How to Frame Walls with Steel Studs

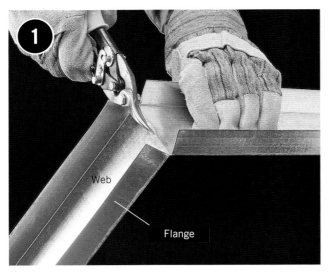

Mark the wall location on the floor or ceiling, following the same procedure used for a wood-frame wall. Cut the top and bottom tracks to length with aviation snips. Cut through the side flanges first, then bend the waste piece back and cut across the web. Use a marker to lay out the tracks with 16" on-center spacing.

Fasten the bottom track to the floor. For wood floors, use 2" coarse-thread drywall screws. For concrete floors, pin the track down with a powder-actuated nailer (see page 121), or use 1¼" masonry screws. Drill pilot holes for screws using a masonry bit. Drive a fastener at each end of the track, then every 24" in between.

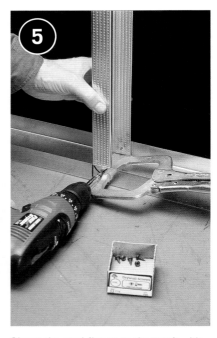

Plumb up from the bottom track with a plumb bob to position the top track. Fasten the top track to the ceiling joists with 1⅝" drywall screws. Drive two screws at each joist location.

At the first stud location, measure between the tracks and cut a stud to length. Insert the stud into the tracks at a slight angle and twist into place. *Note: Cut all subsequent studs from the same end so the punch-outs align.*

Clamp the stud flange to the track with C-clamp pliers and drive a ⁷⁄₁₆" Type S panhead screw through the tracks into the stud. Drive one screw on each side at both ends of the stud. Install remaining studs so the open sides face the same direction (except at door-frame studs).

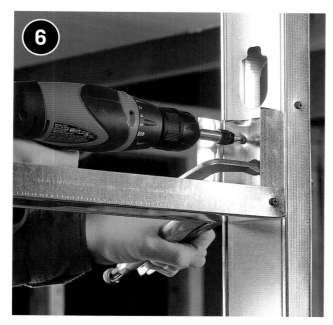

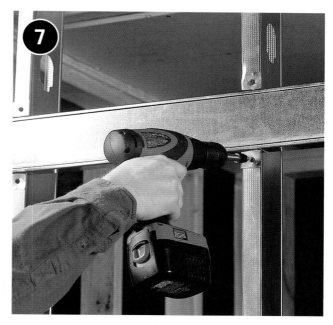

To install a door header, cut the track 8" longer than the opening. Measure in 4" at each end, cut the flanges at an angle toward the mark, then bend down the ends at 90°. Fasten the header in place with three screws at each stud—two through the fastening tab and one through the overlapping flange.

To provide running blocking for cabinets, wainscoting, or other fixtures, snap a chalk line across the face of the studs at the desired height, hold a track level at the line, then notch the flanges of the track to bypass the studs. Fasten the track in place with two screws at each stud location.

 ## STEEL STUD CORNERS & JOINTS

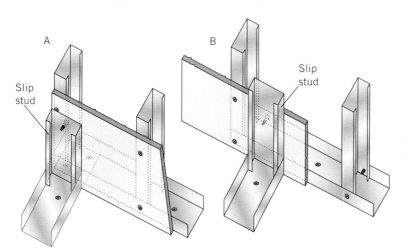

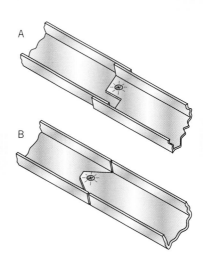

Build corners using a slip stud: A slip stud is not fastened until the adjacent drywall is in place. Form L-shaped corners (A) by overlapping the tracks. Cut off the flange on one side of one track, removing enough to allow room for the overlapping track and drywall. Form a T-shaped corner (B) by leaving a gap between the tracks for the drywall. Secure each slip stud by screwing through the stud into the tracks of the adjacent wall. Also screw through the back side of the drywall into the slip stud, if possible. Where there's no backing behind the slip stud, drive screws at a 45° angle through the back corners of the slip stud and into the drywall.

Join sections with a spliced joint (A) or notched joint (B). Make a spliced joint by cutting a 2" slit in the web of one track. Slip the other track into the slit and secure with a screw. For a notched joint, cut back the flanges of one track and taper the web so it fits into the other track; secure with a screw.

Framing Soffits

Unfinished basements and garages often contain elements like beams, pipes, and ductwork that may be vital to your house but become big obstacles to finishing the space. When you can't conceal the obstructions within walls, and you've determined it's too costly to move them, hide them inside a framed soffit or chase (essentially a vertical soffit). This can also provide a place to run smaller mechanicals, like wiring and water supply lines.

You can frame a soffit with a variety of materials including 2 × 2 lumber and 1⅝" steel studs. Both work well because they're small and lightweight (though steel is usually easier to work with because it's always straight). For large soffits that will house lighting fixtures or other elements, you might want the strength of 2 × 4s or 3⅝" steel studs.

There may be code restrictions about the types of mechanicals that can be grouped together, as well as minimum clearances between the framing and what it encloses. Most codes also specify that soffits, chases, and other framed structures have fireblocking every ten feet and at the intersections between soffits and neighboring walls. Remember too, that drain cleanouts and shutoff valves must be accessible, so you'll need to install access panels at these locations.

Soffits will require an access panel if they house electrical junction boxes or shutoffs for water or gas supply lines. You can plan these into your framing or create them after the wallcovering is installed, as in the framed opening above. Here, a wood frame is glued to the soffit to create support ledges for the removable wallboard cutout.

A soffit is a bump-out that drops down from the ceiling to conceal ductwork, recessed light fixtures and other obstructions.

Variations for Building Soffits

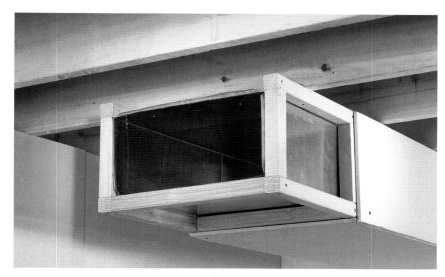

2 × 2 soffit: Build two ladder-like frames for the soffit sides using standard 2 × 2s. Install braces every 16" or 24" to provide nailing support for the edges of the drywall. Attach the side frames to the joists on either side of the obstruction using nails or screws. Then, install crosspieces beneath the obstacle, tying the two sides together.

Simple steel-frame soffit: With ½" drywall, this construction works for soffits up to 16" wide; with ⅝" drywall, up to 24" wide. Use 1⅝, 2½, or 3⅝" steel studs and tracks. Fasten a track to the ceiling and a stud to the adjoining wall using drywall screws. Cut a strip of drywall to form the side of the soffit, and attach a steel stud flush with the bottom edge of the strip using Type S screws. Attach the assembly to the ceiling track, then cut and install drywall panels to form the soffit bottom.

Steel-frame soffit with braces: Use 1⅝, 2½, or 3⅝" steel studs and tracks. Fasten a track to the ceiling and wall with drywall screws. Cut studs to form the side and bottom of the soffit, fasten them to the tracks every 16" or 24" on-center, using Type S panhead screws, then join the pieces with metal angle (you can use a steel track cut in half lengthwise). Use a string line and locking clamps to help keep the frame straight and square during construction.

Installing Drywall

Drywall is inexpensive, perfectly uniform, and easy to install, making it the best choice for do-it-yourselfers working on remodeling projects. But there is a catch. In recent years, builders and homeowners have become aware of a limitation of drywall that has particular bearing on basements: mold and mildew love drywall face paper, which can lead to serious air quality problems in damp basements. To combat this, manufacturers have developed drywall products that resist mold infestation. For basement remodeling, always choose mold-resistant panels.

If you are unable to locate any mold-resistant drywall, the next best choice is moisture-resistant drywall. Commonly called greenboard or blueboard, it is designed to withstand occasional contact with moisture. For areas that will receive tile, use a tile backer or cementboard.

Drywall comes in four-foot-wide panels in lengths ranging from eight to 16 feet and in thicknesses of ¼, ⅜, ½, and ⅝" (although your size choices currently are more limited with mold-resistant drywall). Standard ½" panels are appropriate for walls and for ceilings with sixteen inch on-center framing. Where ceiling framing is 24 inches on-center, ⅝"-thick panels are recommended to prevent sagging.

Hanging drywall is not a task many people look forward to, but it's the stage at which you can see the space come to life.

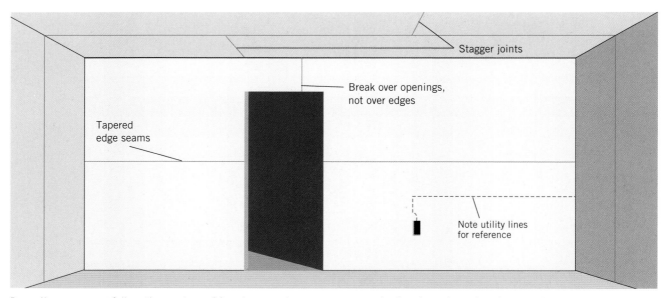

Drywall seams must fall on the centers of framing members, so measure the framing when planning your layout. Use long sheets to span an entire wall, or hang sheets vertically. Avoid butted end joints whenever possible; where they do occur, stagger them between rows so they don't fall on the same framing member. Don't place seams over the corners of doors, windows, and other openings: joints here often crack or cause bulges that interfere with trim. Where framing contains utility lines, draw a map for future reference noting locations of wiring, pipes, and shutoff valves.

Preparation Tips

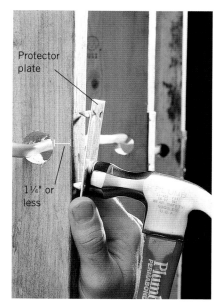

Install protector plates where wires or pipes pass through framing members and are less than 1¼" from the front edge. The plates keep drywall screws from puncturing wires or pipes.

Wrap cold-water pipes along the ceiling with foam insulation before covering them with drywall. This prevents condensation on the pipes that can drip onto the drywall and cause staining.

Mark the location and dimensions of electrical boxes on the floor. This makes it easier to locate them during drywall installation.

Use a plane or chisel on studs that bow slightly. Trim the facing edge just enough so it is flush with the surrounding framing.

Studs in non-load-bearing walls bowed inward more than ¼" can be straightened. Using a handsaw, make a 2" cut into the stud at the midpoint of the bow. Pull the stud outward, and glue a tapered wood shim into the saw cut to hold the stud straight. Attach a 2-ft.-long 2 × 4 brace to one side of the stud to strengthen it, then trim off the shim. For studs that bow outward, plane down the stud surface with a portable power plane or hand plane. Replace any studs that are severely twisted.

How to Make Straight Drywall Cuts

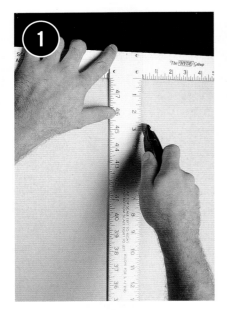  

Mark the length on the face of the panel, then set a T-square at the mark. Hold the square in place with your hand and foot, and cut through the face paper using a utility knife with sharp blade.

Bend the scored section backward with both hands to snap the gypsum core.

Fold back the waste piece and cut through the back paper with the utility knife.

 # How to Cut Notches

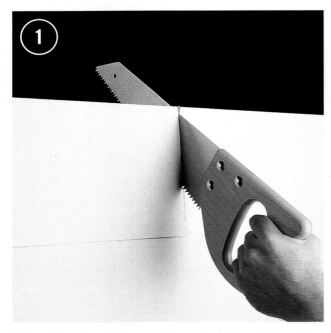 

Using a large drywall saw, cut the vertical sides of the notch. (These saws are also handy for cutting out door and window openings after the drywall is installed.)

Cut the face paper along the bottom of the notch using a utility knife. Snap the waste piece backward to break the core, then cut through the back paper.

How to Cut Large Openings

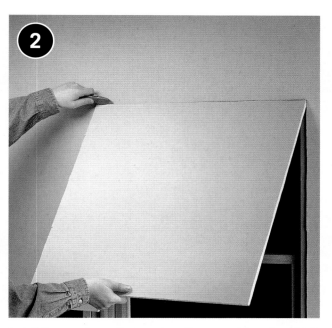

Measure the location of the cutout and transfer the dimensions to the backside of the panel. Score along the line that represents the header of the opening using a straightedge and utility knife.

Install the panel over the opening. The scored line should fall at the header. Cut the drywall along the jambs and up to the header using a drywall saw. Snap forward the waste piece to break the core, then cut through the face paper and remove.

 # How to Mark & Cut Electrical Box Openings

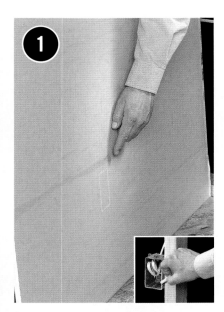

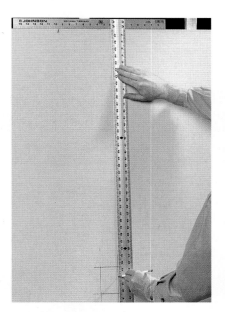

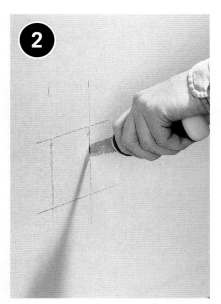

Use chalk or lipstick to rub the front edge of the electrical box (inset) and then position the drywall panel and press it against the box to mark the opening.

Variation: Take measurements and plot out the coordinates onto the drywall sheet.

Drill a pilot hole in one corner of the outline, then make the cutout with a key hole saw.

Hanging Drywall

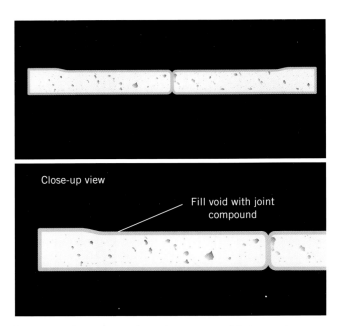

Where untapered panel ends will be butted together, bevel-cut the outside edges of each panel at 45°, removing about ⅛" of material. This helps prevent the paper from creating a ridge along the seam. Peel off any loose paper from the edge.

Butt tapered edges together wherever possible to create a shallow trough for joint compound and drywall seam tape.

Close-up view

Fill void with joint compound

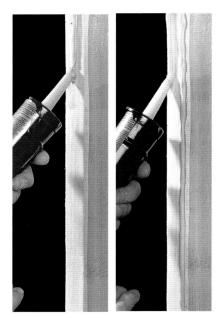

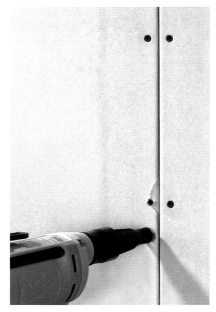

Adhesives create stronger bonds than fasteners and reduce the number of screws needed for panel installation. Apply a ⅜" bead along framing members, stopping 6" from the panel edges (left). At butt joints, apply beads to both sides of the joint (right). Panels are then fastened along the perimeter.

At panel edges, drive fasteners ⅜" from the edges, making sure to hit the framing squarely. If the fastener tears the paper or crumbles the edge, drive another about 2" away from the first.

Recess all screws to provide a space, called a dimple, for the joint compound. However, driving a screw too far and breaking the paper renders it useless. If this happens, drive another screw about 2" away.

How to Hang Drywall on Ceilings

Snap a chalk line perpendicular to the joists, 48⅛" from the starting wall.

Measure to make sure the first panel will break on the center of a joist. If necessary, cut the panel on the end that abuts the side wall so the panel breaks on the next farthest joist. Load the panel onto a rented drywall lift, or use a helper, and lift the panel flat against the joists.

Position the panel with the leading edge on the chalk line and the end centered on a joist. Fasten the panel with 1¼" drywall screws every 8" along edges and 12" in field.

After the first row of panels is installed, begin the next row with a half-panel. This ensures that the butted end joints will be staggered between rows.

 **TIP**

Drywall stilts bring you within reach of ceilings, so you can fasten and finish the drywall without a ladder. Stilts are commonly available at rental centers and are surprisingly easy to use.

How to Hang Drywall on Walls

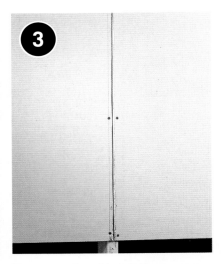

Measure from the wall end or corner to make sure the first panel will break on the center of the stud. If necessary, trim the sheet on the side or end that will be placed in the corner. Mark the stud centers on the panel face and pre-drive screws at each location along the top edge to facilitate fastening. Apply adhesive to the studs, if necessary.

With a helper or a drywall lift, hoist the first panel tight against the ceiling, making sure the side edge is centered on a stud. Push the panel flat against the framing and drive the starter screws to secure the panel. Make any cutouts, then fasten the field of the panel.

Measure, cut, and install the remaining panels along the upper wall. Bevel panel ends slightly, leaving a ⅛" gap between them at the joint. Butt joints can also be installed using back blocking to create a recess.

Wallboard lifter

Measure, cut, and install the bottom row, butting the panels tight to the upper row and leaving a ½" gap at the floor. Secure to the framing along the top edge using the starter screws, then make all cutouts before fastening the rest of the panel.

Variation: When installing drywall vertically, cut each panel so it's ½" shorter than the ceiling height to allow for expansion. (The gap will be covered by base molding.) Avoid placing tapered edges at outside corners, which makes them difficult to finish.

Managing Corners

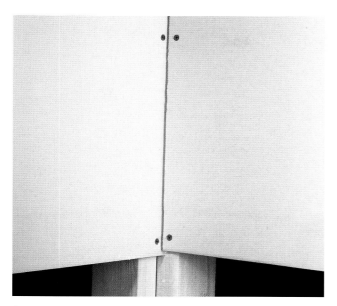

Standard 90° inside corners are installed with the first panel butted against the framing and the adjacent panel butted against the first. The screw spacing remains the same as on a flat wall.

Use a "floating corner" to reduce the chances of popped fasteners and cracks. Install the first panel, fastening only to within one stud bay of the corner. Push the leading edge of the adjacent panel against the first to support the unfastened edge. Fasten the second panel normally, including the corner.

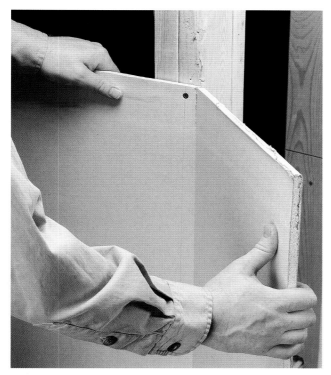

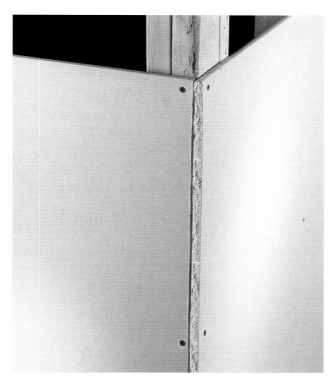

At outside corners, run panels long so they extend past the corner framing. Fasten the panel in place, then score the backside and snap cut to remove the waste piece.

For standard 90° outside corners, install the first panel so the outside edge is flush with the framing, then install the adjacent panel so it overlaps the end of the first panel.

Finishing Drywall

Finishing drywall is the more difficult phase of surfacing walls and ceilings, but it's a project well within the ability of any homeowner. Corner bead is the angle strip, usually made of metal or vinyl, that covers a wallboard corner, creating a straight, durable edge where walls intersect. Most corner beads are installed over the wallboard and are finished with compound. In addition to standard 90° outside-corner bead, there are other bead types designed for specific situations. There are beads for inside corners, flexible beads for off-angles and curves, J-beads and L-beads for flat panel edges, and bullnose beads for creating rounded inside and outside corners.

Joint tape is combined with joint compound to create a permanent layer that covers the wallboard seams, as well as small holes and gaps. There are two types of joint tape—paper and self-adhesive fiberglass mesh.

Joint compound, commonly called mud, seals and levels all seams, corners, and depressions in a wallboard installation. It's also used for skim-coating and some texturing treatments. Joint compound usually takes about 24 hours to dry completely. Available in convenient premixed one- and five-gallon resealable buckets, compound is highly workable and consistent.

TOOLS + MATERIALS

Corner bead	Compound hawk (optional)
Vinyl adhesive (optional)	Pole sander
Staple gun and staples (optional)	220- and 150-grit sandpaper
Joint tape	6-mil plastic sheeting
Joint compound	Painter's tape
Putty knife	Sanding sponge
Taping knife	
Corner knife (optional)	

How to Install Corner Bead

Metal bead: Start from the top and screw metal corner bead flanges in to the drywall with 1¼" drywall screws driven every 9". Alternate sides with each screw to keep the bead centered. Use full lengths wherever possible, or cut two lengths to size so that they butt together. Ensure the ends and spine are aligned.

Vinyl bead: Cut the bead to length and test fit. Spray vinyl adhesive evenly along the length of the corner, then along the inside of the bead. Press the bead into place and fasten it with ½" staples every 8".

How to Tape & Mud

Using a 4 or 6" taping knife, apply compound over each screw head, forcing it into the depression. Firmly drag the knife in the opposite direction, removing excess compound from the panel surface.

Apply an even bed layer of compound about ⅛" thick and 6" wide over tapered seams using a 6" taping knife.

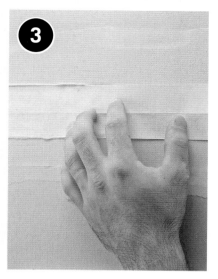

Center the tape over the seam and lightly embed it in the compound, making sure the tape is smooth and straight. At the end of the seam, tear off the tape so it extends all the way into the inside corners and up to the corner bead at outside corners.

Smooth the tape with the taping knife, working out from the center. Apply enough pressure to force compound from underneath the tape, so the tape is flat and has a thin layer beneath it.

At inside corners, smooth the final bit of tape by reversing the knife and carefully pushing it toward the corner. Carefully remove excess compound along the edges of the bed layer with the taping knife.

Cover vertical butt seams with a ⅛"-thick layer of joint compound. You should try and avoid this kind of joint, but in some cases there is no way around it. Cover the compound with seam tape and more compound. Make the taped area extra wide so you can feather it back gradually.

(continued)

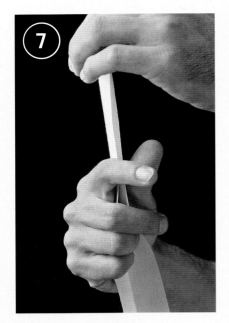

Fold precreased paper tape in half to create a 90° angle to tape inside corners.

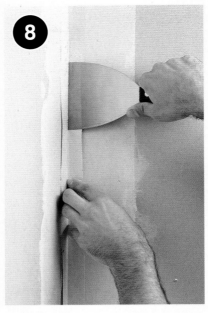

Apply an even layer of compound about ⅛" thick and 3" wide, to both sides of the corner, using a 4" taping knife. Embed the tape into the compound using your fingers and a taping knife.

Carefully smooth and flatten both sides of the tape, removing excess compound to leave only a thin layer beneath. Make sure the center of the tape is aligned straight with the corner.

TIP

An inside corner knife can embed both sides of the tape in one pass—draw the knife along the tape, applying enough pressure to leave a thin layer of compound beneath. Feather each side using a straight 6" taping knife, if necessary.

Finish outside corner bead with a 6" knife. Apply the compound while dragging the knife along the raised spine of the bead. Make a second pass to feather the outside edge of the compound, then a third dragging along the bead again. Smooth any areas where the corner bead meets taped corners or seams.

Scrape off any remaining ridges and chunks after the taping coat has dried completely, then second-coat the screw heads, using a 6" taping knife.

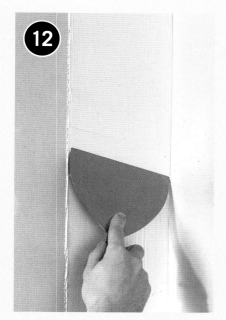

Apply an even layer of compound to both sides of each inside corner using a 6" taping knife. Smooth one side at a time, holding the blade about 15° from horizontal and lightly dragging the point along the corner. Make a second pass to remove excess compound along the outer edges. Repeat, if necessary.

Coat tapered seams with an even layer of all-purpose compound using a 12" taping knife. Whenever possible, apply the coat in one direction and smooth it in the opposite. Feather the sides of the compound first, holding the blade almost flat and applying pressure to the outside of the blade so the blade just skims over the center of the seam.

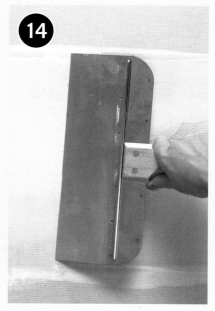

After feathering both side edges of the compound, make a pass down the center of the seam, applying even pressure to the blade. This pass should leave the seam smooth and even, with the edges feathered out to nothing. The joint tape should be completely covered.

Second-coat the outside corners, one side at a time, using a 12" knife. Apply an even layer of compound, then feather the outside edge by applying pressure to the outside of the knife—enough so that the blade flexes and removes most of the compound along the edge but leaves the corner intact. Make a second pass with the blade riding along the raised spine, applying even pressure.

After the filler coat has dried, lightly sand all of the joints, then third-coat the screws. Apply the final coat, following the same steps used for the filler coat but do the seams first, then the outside corners, followed by the inside corners. Use a 12" knife and spread the compound a few inches wider than the joints in the filler coat. Remove most of the compound, filling scratches and low spots but leaving only traces elsewhere. Make several passes, if necessary, until the surface is smooth and there are no knife tracks or other imperfections. Carefully blend intersecting joints so there's no visible transition.

How to Sand Joint Compound

Use sheet plastic and painter's tape to help confine dust to the work area. Cover all doorways, cabinets, built-ins, and any gaps or other openings with plastic, sealing all four edges with tape, otherwise the fine dust produced by sanding can find its way through.

Knockdown any ridges, chunks or tool marks prior to sanding, using a 6" taping knife. Do not apply too much pressure—you don't want to dig into the compound, only remove the excess.

As you work, if you oversand or discover low spots that require another coat of compound, mark the area with a piece of tape for repair after you finish sanding. Make sure to wipe away dust so the tape sticks to the surface.

Lightly sand all seams and outside corners using a pole sander with 220-grit sanding screen or 150-grit sandpaper. Work in the direction of the joints, applying even pressure to smooth transitions and high areas. Don't sand out depressions; fill them with compound and resand. Be careful not to over-sand or expose joint tape.

Inside corners often are finished with only one or two thin coats of compound over the tape. Sand the inside edge of joints only lightly and smooth the outside edge carefully; inside corners will be sanded by hand later.

Fine-sand the seams, outside corners, and fastener heads using a sanding block with 150- to 220-grit sanding screen or sandpaper. As you work, use your hand to feel for defects along the compound. A bright work light angled to highlight seams can help reveal problem areas.

To avoid damage from oversanding, use a 150-grit dry sanding sponge to sand inside corners. The sides of sanding sponges also contain grit, allowing you to sand both sides of a corner at once to help prevent oversanding.

For tight or hard-to-reach corners, fold a piece of sanding screen or sandpaper in thirds and sand the area carefully. Rather than using just your fingertips, try to flatten your hand as much as possible to spread out the pressure to avoid sanding too deep.

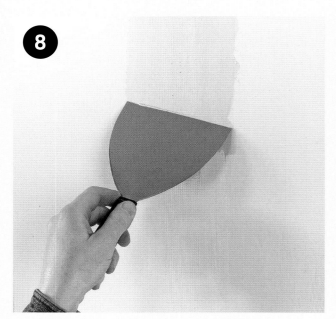

Repair depressions, scratches, or exposed tape due to oversanding after final sanding is complete. Wipe the area with a dry cloth to remove dust, then apply a thin coat of compound. Allow to dry thoroughly, then resand.

With sanding complete, remove dust from the panels with a dry towel or soft broom. Use a wet-dry vacuum to clean out all electrical boxes and around floors, windows, and doors, then carefully roll up sheet plastic and discard. Finally, damp mop the floor to remove any remaining dust.

Installing a Suspended Ceiling

Suspended options are traditionally popular ceiling for basements and some garages because they hang below pipes and other mechanicals, providing easy access to them. Suspended ceiling tile manufacturers offer a wide array of ceiling tiles from which to choose. Popular styles mimic historical tin tiles and add depth to the ceiling while minimizing sound and vibration noise.

A suspended ceiling is a grid framework made of lightweight metal brackets hung on wires attached to ceiling or floor joists. The frame consists of T-shaped main beams (mains), cross tees (tees), and L-shaped wall angles. The grid supports ceiling panels, which rest on the flanges of the framing pieces. Panels are available in 2 × 2-ft. or 2 × 4-ft., in a variety of styles. Special options include insulated panels, acoustical panels that absorb sound, and light-diffuser screens for use with fluorescent lights. Generally, metal-frame ceiling systems are more durable than ones made of plastic.

To begin your ceiling project, devise the panel layout based on the size of the room, placing equally sized trimmed panels on opposite sides to create a balanced look. Your ceiling must also be level.

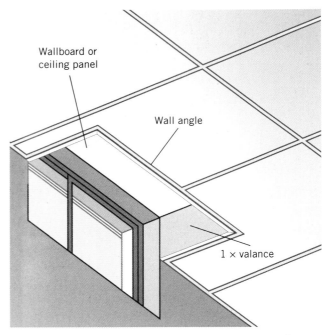

Build a valance around basement awning windows so they can be opened fully. Attach 1× lumber of an appropriate width to joists or blocking. Install drywall (or a suspended-ceiling panel trimmed to fit) to the joists inside the valance.

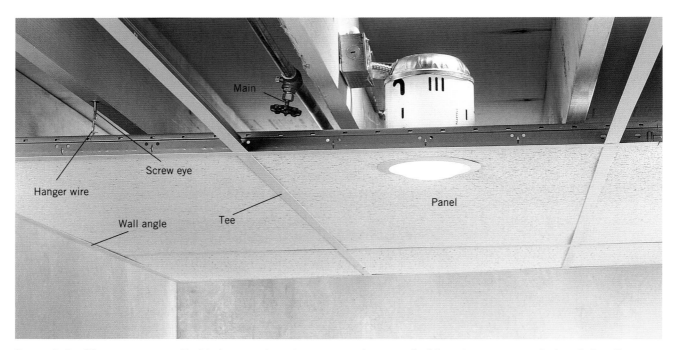

Suspended ceilings are very practical in basements and garages, and you can find them in many more design choices than you might expect.

How to Install a Suspended Ceiling

Make a mark on one wall that represents the ceiling height plus the height of the wall angle. Use a water level to transfer that height to both ends of each wall. Snap a chalk line to connect the marks. This line represents the top of the ceiling's wall angle.

Attach wall angle pieces to the studs on all walls, positioning the top of the wall angle flush with the chalk line. Use 1½" drywall screws (or short masonry nails driven into mortar joints on concrete block walls). Cut angle pieces using aviation snips.

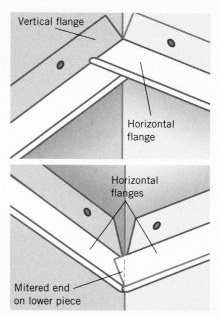

Vertical flange

Horizontal flange

Horizontal flanges

Mitered end on lower piece

Tip: Trim wall angle pieces to fit around corners. At inside corners (top), back-cut the vertical flanges slightly, then overlap the horizontal flanges. At outside corners (bottom), miter-cut one horizontal flange and overlap the flanges.

Mark the location of each main on the wall angles at the ends of the room. The mains must be parallel to each other and perpendicular to the ceiling joists. Set up a guide string for each main using a thin string and lock-type clamps (inset). Clamp the strings to the opposing wall angles, stretching them very taut so there's no sagging.

Install screw eyes for hanging the mains using a drill and screw eye driver. Drill pilot holes and drive the eyes into the joists every 4 ft., locating them directly above the guide strings. Attach hanger wire to the screw eyes by threading one end through the eye and twisting the wire on itself at least three times. Trim excess wire, leaving a few inches of wire hanging below the level of the guide string.

(continued)

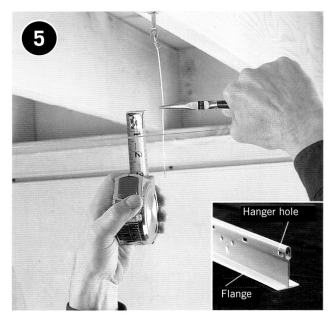

Measure the distance from the bottom of a main's flange to the hanger hole in the web (inset). Use this measurement to prebend each hanger wire. Measure up from the guide string and make a 90° bend in the wire using pliers.

Hanger hole

Flange

Following your ceiling plan, mark the placement of the first tee on opposite wall angles at one end of the room. Set up a guide string for the tee using a string and clamps, as before. This string must be perpendicular to the guide strings for the mains.

Tee slot

Trim one end of each main so that a tee slot in the main's web is aligned with the tee guide string, and the end of the main bears fully on a wall angle. Set the main in place to check the alignment of the tee slot with the string.

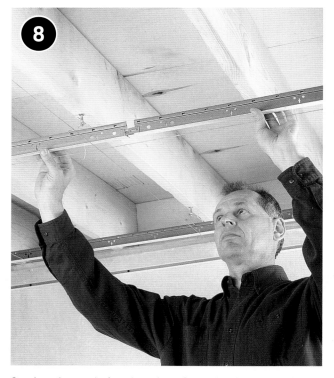

Cut the other end of each main to fit, so that it rests on the opposing wall angle. If a single main cannot span the room, splice two mains together end-to-end (the ends should be fashioned with male-female connectors). Make sure the tee slots remain aligned when splicing.

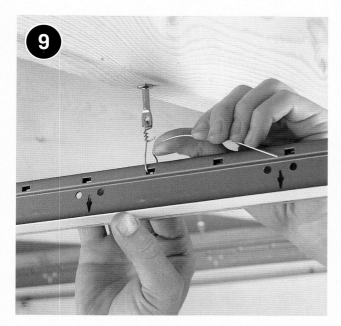

Install the mains by setting the ends on the wall angle and threading the hanger wires through the hanger holes in the webs. The wires should be as close to vertical as possible. Wrap each wire around itself three times, making sure the main's flange is level with the main guide string. Also install a hanger near each main splice.

Attach tees to the mains, slipping the tabbed ends into the tee slots on the mains. Align the first row of tees with the tee guide string; install the remaining rows at 4-ft. intervals. If you're using 2 × 2-ft. panels, install 2-ft. cross tees between the midpoints of the 4-ft. tees. Cut and install the border tees, setting the tee ends on the wall angles. Remove all guide strings and clamps.

Place full ceiling panels into the grid first, then install the border panels. Lift the panels in at an angle, and position them so they rest on the frame's flanges. Reach through adjacent openings to adjust the panels, if necessary.

To trim the border panels to size, cut them face-up using a straightedge and utility knife.

Windows, Doors + Trim

Basement and garage windows and doors may look like what you'd find elsewhere in the house, but they are really a breed apart. For instance, there is often less flexibility with basement openings, because it can be much more difficult, or even impossible, to change the dimensions of a window or door serving a basement. Garage doors and windows often have to be installed in shallower walls that were originally framed with 2 × 4s.

More importantly, function must—for safety and code compliance—lead when it comes to choosing, changing, or installing new windows or doors in a basement. The paramount issue is always egress. As a matter of safety, it's essential that any windows or doors allow for easy and safe passage in the event of an emergency. That may translate to anything from widening an existing narrow door opening, to adding a climb-out window well. In garages, the key issues are light penetration (which is why "windows" includes the option for a skylight) and ventilation.

Although those concerns come first and foremost, there's no reason to sacrifice style for safety or function. There is a vast range of design options for basement and garage openings, and the trim you choose can be the icing on the cake.

In this chapter:

- Installing an Egress Window
- Replacing Basement Windows
- Trimming Basement Windows
- Installing Prehung Interior Doors
- Installing Pocket Doors
- Installing Bifold Doors
- Installing Walkout Patio Doors
- Installing Molding

Installing an Egress Window

An egress window brings a pleasant source of natural light and ventilation to a dark, dank basement. More importantly, it can provide a lifesaving means of escape in the event of a fire. Before you proceed with this project, read more about building code issues regarding basement egress on page 27. Contact your local building department to apply for the proper permits and to learn more about the code requirements for your area.

As long as the window opens wide enough to meet minimum standards for egress, the particular window style is really up to you. Casement windows are ideal, because they crank open quickly and provide unobstructed escape. A tall, double-hung window or wide sliding window can also work. Select a window with insulated glass and clad with vinyl or aluminum for durability; it will be subject to humidity and temperature fluctuations just like any other above-grade window in your home.

TOOLS + MATERIALS

Tape measure	Gloves
4-ft. level	Window well and window
Stakes and string line	Pea gravel
Shovel	Plastic sheeting
Colored masking tape	Self-tapping masonry screws
Hammer drill with ½" dia. × 12- to 16"-long masonry bit	2× pressure-treated lumber
Masonry saw	Shims
Hand maul	Insulation materials
Cold chisel	Concrete sleeve anchors
Trowel	Quick-curing concrete
Miter saw	3½" deck screws
Hammer	Foam backer rod
Drill/driver, hammer	Tamper
Caulk and caulk gun	

The second fundamental component of a basement egress window project is the subterranean escape well you install outside the foundation. There are several options to choose from: prefabricated well kits made of lightweight plastic that bolt together and are easy to install; corrugated metal wells that are a lower-cost option; or, a well built from scratch using concrete, stone, or landscape timber.

Installing an egress window involves four major steps: digging the well, cutting a new or larger window opening in the foundation, installing the window, and, finally, installing the well. You'll save time and effort if you hire a backhoe operator to excavate the well. In most cases, you'll also need a large concrete saw (available at most rental stores) to cut the foundation wall.

Replacing a small basement window with an egress window is a big job, but it is required if you want to convert part of a basement into livable space, especially a bedroom.

How to Install an Egress Window + Window Well

Lay out the border of the window well area with stakes and string. Plan the length and width of the excavation to be several feet larger than the window well's overall size to provide extra room for installation and adjustment.

Excavate the well to a depth 6 to 12" deeper than the well's overall height to allow room for drainage gravel. Make sure to have your local public utilities inspect the well excavation area and okay it for digging before you start.

Measure and mark the foundation wall with brightly colored masking tape to establish the overall size of the window's rough opening (here, we're replacing an existing window). Be sure to take into account the window's rough opening dimensions, the thickness of the rough framing (usually 2× stock), and the width of the structural header you may need to build. Remember also that sill height must be within 44" of the floor. Remove existing wall coverings inside the layout area.

If the floor joists run perpendicular to your project wall, build a temporary support wall parallel to the foundation wall and 6 to 8 ft. from it. Staple sheet plastic to the wall and floor joists to form a work tent that will help control concrete dust.

(continued)

Drill reference holes at each bottom corner with a hammer drill and long masonry bit. These holes will provide reference points for cutting from both sides, ensuring clean breaks.

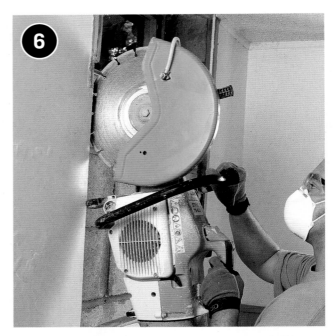

Equip a masonry cutting saw (or large angle grinder) with a diamond blade and set it for a ½" cut to score the blocks first. Then reset the saw to full depth and make the final bottom and side cuts through the blocks. Wear a tight-fitting particle mask, ear and eye protection, and gloves for all of this cutting work; the saw will generate a tremendous amount of thick dust. Feed the saw slowly and steadily. Stop and rest periodically so the dust can settle.

On the outside foundation wall, score the cuts, then make full-depth cuts.

Strike the blocks with a hand maul to break or loosen the block sections. When all the blocks are removed, carefully chip away remaining debris with a cold chisel to create flat surfaces.

Fill the hollow voids in concrete block walls, with broken pieces of block, then level and smooth the voids by trowelling on a fresh layer of quick-curing concrete. Flatten the surfaces, and allow the concrete to dry overnight.

If your project requires a new header above the new window, build it from pieces of 2× lumber sandwiching ½" plywood and fastened together with construction adhesive and 10d nails. Slip it into place and tack it temporarily to the mudsill with 3½" deck screws driven toenail style.

Cut the sill plate for the window's rough frame from 2× treated lumber that's the same width as the thickness of the foundation wall. Fasten the sill to the foundation with ³⁄₁₆ × 3¼" countersunk masonry screws. Drill pilot holes for the screws first with a hammer drill.

Cut two pieces of treated lumber just slightly longer than the opening so they'll fit tightly between the new header and sill. Tap them into place with a maul. Adjust them for plumb and fasten them to the foundation with countersunk masonry screws or powder-actuated fasteners.

(continued)

Apply a thick bead of silicone caulk around the outside edges of the rough frame and set the window in its opening, seating the nailing flanges into the caulk. Shim the window so the frame is level and plumb. Test the action of the window to make sure the shims aren't bowing the frame.

Attach the window's nailing flanges to the rough frame with screws or nails, as specified by the manufacturer. Check the window action periodically as you fasten it to ensure that it still operates smoothly.

Seal gaps between the rough frame and the foundation with a bead of exterior silicone or polyurethane caulk. If the gaps are wider than ¼", insert a piece of backer rod first, then cover it with caulk. On the interior, fill gaps around the window shims with strips of foam backer rod, fiberglass insulation, or a bead of minimally expanding spray foam. Do not distort the window frame.

Fill the well excavation with 6 to 12" of pea gravel. This will serve as the window's drain system. Follow the egress well kit instructions to determine the exact depth required; you may need to add more gravel so the top of the well will be above the new window. *Note: We added a drain down to the foundation's perimeter tile for improved drainage as well.*

Set the bottom section of the well into the hole, and position it evenly from left to right relative to the window. Adjust the gravel surface to level the well section carefully.

Stack the second well section on top of the first, and connect the two with the appropriate fasteners.

Fasten the window well sections to the foundation wall with concrete sleeve anchors driven into prebored pilot holes. You could also use masonry nails driven with a powder-actuated tool.

When all the well sections are assembled and secured, nail pieces of trim around the window frame to hide the nailing flange. Complete the well installation by using excavated dirt to backfill around the outside of the well. Pack the soil with a tamper, creating a slope for good drainage. If you are installing a window well cover, set it in place and fasten it according to the manufacturer's instructions. The cover must be removable.

Replacing Basement + Garage Windows

Upgrading existing windows in a basement or garage is often a necessity, given that these spaces often begin life as purely functional storage and utility facilities. That's why the windows in most basements and garages are afterthoughts, and a renovated space can be greatly improved with replacement units.

There are three basic considerations in choosing a basement window: egress, ventilation, and sunlight penetration. (The last two are the primary considerations for replacement garage windows). If the window opening is too small for physical passage and can't be enlarged because of structural concerns, egress may not figure into your choice. All windows, however, should facilitate movement of light and air into the redesigned basement or garage.

There is, however, one more consideration—window style. This includes the opening mechanism, material used to construct the window frame, and the molding you use to trim the window. Frame material will have the greatest impact on cost, functionality, and looks. Here are the window frame materials from which you'll choose:

• **Vinyl.** This is the most popular type of replacement thanks to its combination of durability and affordability. Energy efficient and moisture and rot-resistant, even mid-range vinyl windows can last more than 15 years. Be aware, however, that these windows don't take paint well. That's why white is the most common vinyl window frame color, and it is something to consider if you plan on painting the exterior of a garage with an unusual color scheme.

• **Fiberglass.** Stronger and longer-lasting than vinyl (as well as more expensive), fiberglass windows are paintable and can be formed into different textures, including wood grain. The material resists moisture, but the finish may become chalky after long exposure to direct sunlight.

• **Composite.** Long used for outdoor decking, composite materials are now a growing category of window frames. This extruded material can be convincingly fabricated to look like wood or metal, is as durable as vinyl and almost as inexpensive. Long-lasting, moisture-resistant, and tough, the material is also paintable.

As this window shows, even egress windows inside a window well can be significant sources of light. This one is also paired with an identical unit on the opposite wall, allowing for cross ventilation.

• **Wood.** This is considered a luxury window material, but it requires regular upkeep not only to remain as attractive as possible, but also to protect the framing. Wood is susceptible to moisture and insect infiltration, mold, mildew, and rot. The material is, however, paintable and stainable, offering a vast number of possibilities for the final appearance.

• **Aluminum.** Not recommended for high-humidity applications, but if your basement or garage is dry, and local weather is dry and temperate, these chic architectural style windows may be right for you. They are strong and lightweight, allowing for larger glass surfaces than other window units of the same size. They are, however, pricey.

TOOLS + MATERIALS

Tape measure	Hammer or nail gun
Large screwdriver or pry bar	Minimal expanding spray foam
Powder-actuated tool and cartridges	Work gloves
New window	Safety glasses
Torpedo level	Molding
Wood shims	Circular saw
2" wood screws	Paint or stain
Drill and bits	Paintbrush

Basement + Garage Replacement-Window Styles

The styles here are the most common. Home centers and window sellers usually offer windows in a standard 32" width, at heights of 13", 15", 17", or 23". However, many homeowners are either dealing with unusual dimensions in the existing windows, or want to change the dimensions to enlarge the openings.

That's easy enough by having the window custom-made to the preferred dimensions—an option that is far less expensive that one might think. You can also adapt the frame dimensions to a standard size by building out the frame with thicker pieces of lumber.

Double/Single Hung. This classic window style is attractive and may match existing windows in the home. Single-hung windows open only from the bottom, while double-hung open from the bottom up, and top down. These can be good choices to maintain continuity of style between the house and the garage.

Casement. A casement window opens by way of a crank outward. This style offers the largest area of passage of any type, but the exterior window well must be deep enough to allow for the window to open fully. It is a simple and pleasing look that is not usually used in garages because the open window impedes passage outside.

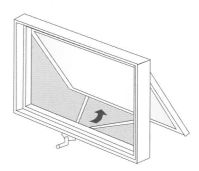

Awning (transom). The awning window—also called a transom—is usually used only for smaller windows, such as the clerestory windows at the top of the walls in some basements. The single sash is hinged from the top, opening from the bottom. This can be good for ventilation, but these windows are not used for egress.

Fixed. As the name indicates, the sash in this type of window does not open. Although these are less expensive than operable windows—and less prone to failure due to wear and tear—they are best used where egress is already established elsewhere in the basement, and where there is a premium on energy efficiency. Usually it's best for small openings that would not be essential to egress or ventilation.

Bypass. This version involves a moving sash that slides open in front of a fixed sash (essentially a horizontal version of the single-hung window). These are great for ventilation, even in smaller openings, but tend to allow for limited egress unless the opening is already fairly large. They can be excellent low-cost choices for garages, especially if the house itself is equipped with bypass units.

BEFORE

AFTER

Basement windows are the only source of natural light, but they also can allow cold air or even intruders to enter. If you are remodeling your basement, it makes sense to update old windows with new ones that offer better energy efficiency and security.

How to Replace a Basement or Garage Window

1

2

Remove the old window and inspect the rough frame. If it shows signs of rot, remove the frame by cutting the sill and header in half and prying the halves out. Cut new frame members from pressure-treated dimension lumber.

Install the new rough frame using a powder-actuated tool to drive masonry nails. Apply several thick beads of caulk to the concrete surfaces first to create a good seal. The header and sill should run the full width of the opening and be installed before the side members. Caulk around the frame edges and paint the frame with exterior primer.

Position the new window unit in the opening and test it with a level. Use shims to raise it so it is not resting on the sill. Adjust it so the gaps are even on the sides. *Tip: You may find it easier to adjust and install the window frame if you remove the glass sash first.*

Attach the window frame to the rough frame opening with screws driven through the jambs. Often, the screw is accessed through a hole in the inner jamb layer. Arrange shims so the screws will pass through them. Do not overdrive screws—it can pull the window frame out of square.

Fill gaps between the rough window frame and the new window unit with minimal expanding spray foam. Do not spray in too much—it can distort the frame when it dries.

Install stop molding on both sides of the window to cover gaps between the window and the rough frame. Paint the stop molding and frame to match your trim color.

Trimming Basement Windows

Basement windows bring much-needed sunlight into dark areas, but even in finished basements they often get ignored on the trim front. This is partly because most basement foundation walls are at least eight inches thick, and often a lot thicker. Add a furred-out wall and the window starts to look more like a tunnel with a pane of glass at the end. But with some well-designed and well-executed trim carpentry, you can turn the depth disadvantage into a positive.

A basement window opening may be finished with wallboard, but the easiest way to trim one is by making extra-wide custom jambs that extend from the inside face of the window frame to the interior wall surface. Because of the extra width, plywood stock is a good choice for the custom jambs.

The project shown here is created with veneer-core plywood with oak veneer surface. The jamb members are fastened together into a nice square frame using rabbet joints at the corner. The frame is scribed and installed as a single unit and then

trimmed out with oak casing. The casing is applied flush with the inside edges of the frame opening. If you prefer to have a reveal edge around the interior edge of the casing, you will need to add a solid hardwood strip to the edge of the frame so the plies of the plywood are not visible.

TOOLS + MATERIALS

Pencil

Tape measure

Table saw

Drill and bits

2-ft. level

Framing square

Utility knife

Straightedge

Finish-grade ¾" oak plywood

Spray-foam insulation

1¼" composite or cedar wood shims

2" finish nails

1⅝" drywall screws

Carpenter's glue

Because they are set into thick foundation walls, basement windows present a bit of a trimming challenge. But the thickness of the foundation wall also lets you create a handy ledge that's deep enough to hold potted plants or even sunning cats.

How to Trim a Basement Window

Check to make sure the window frame and surrounding area are dry and free of rot, mold, or damage. At all four corners of the basement window, measure from the inside edges of the window frame to the wall surface. Add 1" to the longest of these measurements.

Set your table saw to make a rip cut to the width arrived at in step 1. If you don't have a table saw, set up a circular saw and straightedge cutting guide to cut strips to this length. With a fine-tooth panel-cutting blade, rip enough plywood strips to make the four jamb frame components.

Miter gauge

Crosscut the plywood strips to correct lengths. In our case, we designed the jamb frame to be the exact same outside dimensions as the window frame, since there was some space between the jamb frame and the rough opening.

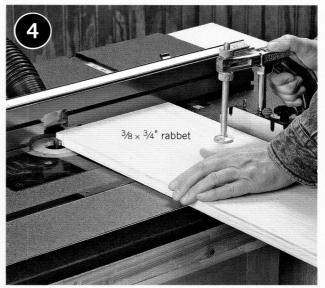

3⁄8 × 3⁄4" rabbet

Cut ⅜"-deep × ¾"-wide rabbets at each end of the head jamb and the sill jamb. A router table is the best tool for this job, but you may use a table saw or handsaws and chisels. Inspect the jambs first and cut the rabbets in whichever face is in better condition. To ensure uniformity, we ganged the two jambs together (they're the same length). It's also a good idea to include backer boards to prevent tearout.

(continued)

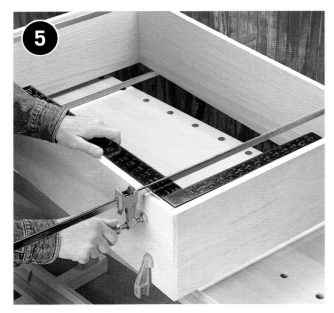

Glue and clamp the frame parts together, making sure to clamp near each end from both directions. Use a carpenter's square inside the frame to check if the frame is square.

Before the glue sets, carefully drill three perpendicular pilot holes, countersunk, through the rabbeted workpieces and into the side jambs at each corner. Space the pilot holes evenly, keeping the end ones at least ¾" in from the end. Drive a 1⅝" drywall screw into each pilot hole, taking care not to overdrive. Double-check each corner for square as you work, adjusting the clamps if needed.

Let the glue dry for at least one hour (overnight is better), then remove the clamps and set the frame in the window opening. Adjust and shim the frame so it is centered and level in the opening and the exterior-side edges fit flush against the window frame.

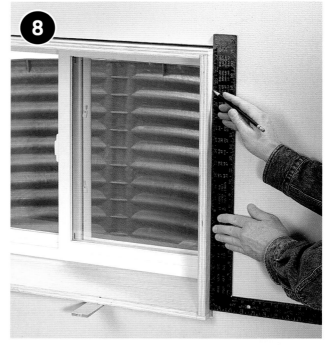

Taking care not to disturb the frame's position (rest a heavy tool on the sill to hold it in place if you wish), press a straight-edge against the wall surface and mark trimming points at the point where the rule meets the jambs at each side of all four frame corners using a sharp pencil.

Remove the frame and clamp it on a flat work surface. Use a straightedge to connect the scribe marks at the ends of each jamb frame side. Set the cutting depth of your circular saw to just a small fraction over ¾". Clamp a straightedge guide to the frame so the saw blade will follow the cutting line and trim each frame side in succession. (The advantage of using a circular saw here is that any tearout from the blade will be on the nonvisible faces of the frame.)

Replace the frame in the window opening in the same orientation as when you scribed it and install shims until it is level and centered in the opening. Drive a few finish nails through the side jambs into the rough frame. Also drive a few nails through the sill jamb. Most trim carpenters do not drive nails into the head jamb.

Insulate between the jamb frame and the rough frame with spray-in polyurethane foam. Look for minimal-expanding foam labeled "window and door" and don't spray in too much. Let the foam dry for a half hour or so and then trim off the excess with a utility knife. *Tip: Protect the wood surfaces near the edges with wide strips of painter's tape.*

Remove the painter's tape and clean up the mess from the foam (there is always some). Install case molding. We used picture-frame techniques to install fairly simple oak casing.

Installing Prehung Interior Doors

Install prehung interior doors after framing is complete and the wallboard has been installed. If the rough opening for the door has been framed accurately, installing the door takes about an hour. Standard prehung doors have 4½"-wide jambs and are sized to fit walls with 2 × 4 construction and half-inch wallboard. If you have 2 × 6 construction or thicker wall surface material, you can special order a door to match, or you can add jamb extensions to a standard-sized door.

One drawback to prehung doors is that they frequently are hollow-core doors, which means that they consist mostly of a couple of thin layers of veneer that sandwich a network of cardboard spacers. This is not necessarily a problem except when you need to shorten the door—a common situation in basements.

TOOLS + MATERIALS

Prehung door unit	Eye protection
Tape measure	Work Gloves
Carpenter's pencil	Wood glue
Sawhorses	Straightedge
Table saw or circular saw	Chisel
Shims	Brads
Level	Drill and bits
Claw hammer	Latch set

 ## How to Shorten a Prehung Door

Draw a straight cutting line at the bottom of the door, not the top. Score along the line with a utility knife and then cut along the line with a circular saw and straightedge guide.

Strip the veneer from the frame rail with a chisel. If you cut through the frame and the top of the door still contains a frame, test it to see how sturdy it is. If there is more than ½" of rail still in the door you can go ahead and rehang the door in the frame.

Apply wood glue to the frame rail once the veneer is removed and insert the rail into the top of the hollow door. Adjust so the rail is flush along the top and let the glue dry before rehanging the door in the jambs (which you will also need to trim).

How to Install a Prehung Door

Unpack your door and remove any braces that are stapled to the jamb to keep the door from swinging in the jamb during transit.

Set the door in the framed opening with the door closed. Shift it so it is centered side to side and the jambs are flush with the wall surface. Check for plumb by placing a level on the hinge-side jamb. Shim as necessary and then open the door—the pressure from the shims should hold the door in place.

Anchor the hinge-side jamb with 8d casing nails driven through the jamb and shims and into the rough frame. If the jambs are made of hardwood such as oak, drill pilot holes for the nails.

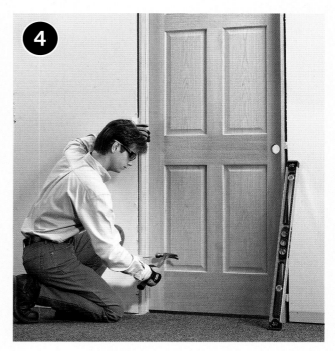

Drive nails near the bottom hinge and then the middle, if your door has three hinges. Make sure to drive through shims. If you drive nails away from the shims the jambs may bow outward.

(continued)

Double-check the jamb on the strike plate side to make sure it is plumb and flush with the wall surface, and then nail it to the framing, nailing through the shims as you did on the hinge jamb.

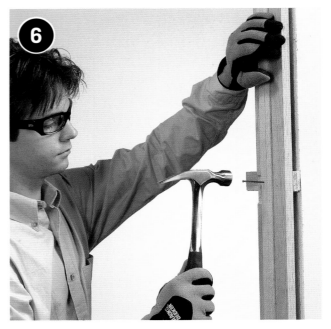

Drive a few nails through pilot holes in the center of the door stop for reinforcement. Locate the nails so they go through shims.

JAMB EXTENSIONS

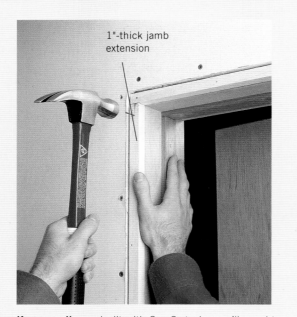

1"-thick jamb extension

If your walls are built with 2 × 6 studs, you'll need to extend the jambs by attaching 1"-thick wood strips to the edges of the jamb after the door is installed. Use glue and 4d casing nails when attaching jamb extensions. Make the strips from the same wood as the jamb.

Attach the preattached case moldings to the framing members with 4d finish nails. Set the nail heads. Fill all nail holes with wood putty and then paint or stain. Use a nail set to recess the nail heads. Install a latch set.

How to Install a Latch Set

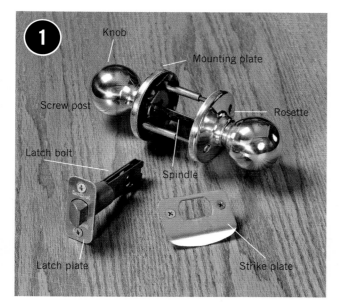

1

Knob
Mounting plate
Screw post
Rosette
Latch bolt
Spindle
Latch plate
Strike plate

A latch set is an interior doorknob set with a latch and strike plate. It is installed in doors that are not intended to be locked. A latch set with a locking mechanism is called a lockset.

2

Insert the latch bolt and latch plate assembly into the hole drilled in the edge of the door and fasten the plate to the door. Make sure the curved side of the end of the latch bolt is facing toward the door. The door edge usually is premortised so the plate is flush. If it is not, you'll need to cut a shallow mortise for the plate with a wood chisel.

3

Insert the spindle attached to one of the knobs through the same-shaped hole in the latch bolt. Hold the knob against the door and slide the other knob in place so the spindle fits into the spindle hole in the second knob.

4

Insert the long post screws into the screw opening and thread them into the screw holes in the opposite knob. Tighten them to draw the two halves of the knob set together. Do not overtighten.

5

Position the strike plate in the mortise in the jamb (cut one with a chisel if your jamb has no mortise). Make sure the latch bolt and the hole in the strike plate are aligned. Attach the strike plate to the jamb with the screw provided by the manufacturer.

Installing Pocket Doors

Pocket doors are a space-saving alternative to traditional hinged interior doors. Swinging doors can monopolize up to 16 square feet of floor space in a basement, which is why pocket doors are a perfect choice for tight spaces, like the rooms in many basements or a divided area in a garage. Installed in pairs, pocket doors can divide large rooms into more intimate spaces and can still be opened to use the entire area.

Pocket door hardware kits generally are universal and can be adapted for almost any interior door. In this project, the frame kit includes an adjustable track, steel-clad split studs, and all the required hanging hardware. The latch hardware, jambs, and the door itself are all sold separately. Pocket door frames can also be purchased as preassembled units that can be easily installed into a rough opening.

Framing and installing a pocket door is not difficult in new construction or a major remodel.

But retrofitting a pocket door in place of a standard door or installing one in a wall without an existing door, is a major project that involves removing the wall material, framing the new opening, installing and hanging the door, and refinishing the wall. Hidden utilities, such as wiring, plumbing, and heating ducts, must be rerouted if encountered.

The rough opening for a pocket door is at least twice the width of a standard door opening. If the wall is load bearing, you will need to install an appropriately sized header.

Because pocket doors are easy to open and close and require no threshold, they offer increased accessibility for wheelchair or walker users, provided the handles are easy to use. If you are installing a pocket door for this purpose, be aware that standard latch hardware may be difficult to use for some individuals.

TOOLS + MATERIALS

Tape measure
Hammer
Nail set
Screwdriver
Level
Drill
Hacksaw
Drywall tools
2 × 4 lumber
8d, and 6d common nails
Chalk line
Pocket door frame kit
Door
1¼" wallboard screws
Drywall materials
8d and 6d finish nails
1½" wood screws
Door casing
Wood finishing materials

Track header
Door track
Track trim board
Split studs
Tri-wheeled hanger
Door bracket
Bumper
Split studs
Door guide

How to Install Pocket Doors

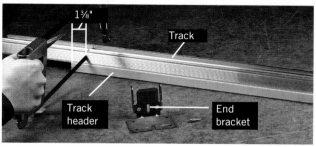

Frame the rough opening for the pocket door according to the manufacturer's sizing instructions. Determine the proper height for the overhead track and drive a nail at each side of the door opening. Leave the nailheads protruding slightly so you can support the track on them temporarily.

Cut the overhead track to length according to the width of the pocket door. The wooden portion of the track should be premarked with cutting lines for standard door sizes (top). The metal part of the track is cut shorter than the wood part. Attach the end brackets to the track after the trim cuts are made.

Position the overhead track in the framed opening, resting the end bracket on the nails driven in step 1 for temporary support. Center the assembly and secure it by driving 8d common nails through the nailing holes in the brackets.

Attach the split studs in the framed opening. Split studs are the secret to pocket doors. They have an open center that allows the door to pass through. Because they are reinforced with steel they can perform structural bearing comparable to a solid wood stud. Nail the split studs to the wooden part of the overhead track.

Fasten split studs to the floor by nailing through the bottom plate into the subfloor. Snap chalk lines aligned with the front and back of the sole plate in the framed opening as guidance.

(continued)

6

Fasten rolling brackets to the top of the door following the spacing recommended by the door manufacturer (usually a couple of inches in from each end). Attach wall coverings around the framed opening, making sure your fasteners are not long enough to protrude into the pocket. *Tip: Paint or stain the door before hanging it.*

7

Tri-wheeled hanger

Lock arm

Hang the door by pressing the bracket up into the tri-wheeled hangers in the overhead track and then snapping the lock arm over the hanger. If you have not installed floor covering yet, do so before proceeding to the trim installation.

8

Attach a full-width door jamb for the door to close against. Nail the jamb to the framed opening stud with 8d casing nails.

9

3/16"

Attach split jambs to the side of the framed opening housing the door. Maintain a gap of 3/16" between the door and the inside edges of the split jambs.

10

Install split head jambs with countersunk wood screws. This allows you to easily remove the head jamb if the door needs to be replaced or removed for repair.

11

Attach the latch and pull hardware, which is usually supplied with the door. Also attach door guide hardware at the wall opening to help track the door. Fill nail holes and finish the jambs and walls.

Installing Bifold Doors

Bifold doors provide easy access to a closet without requiring much clearance for opening, making them ideal for use in the often small sleeping quarters in a basement or garage bedroom. Most home centers stock kits that include two pairs of prehinged doors, a head track, and all the necessary hardware and fasteners. Typically, the doors in these kits have predrilled holes for the pivot and guide posts. Hardware kits are also sold separately for custom projects. There are many types of bifold door styles, read and follow the manufacturer's instructions for the product you use.

TOOLS + MATERIALS

Tape measure	Hacksaw
Level	Prehinged bifold doors
Circular saw	Head track
Straightedge (optional)	Mounting hardware
Drill	Panhead screws
Plane	Flathead screws
Screwdriver	

How to Install Bifold Doors

Cut the head track to the width of the opening using a hacksaw. Insert the roller mounts into the track, then position the track in the opening. Fasten it to the header using panhead screws.

Measure and mark each side jamb at the floor for the anchor bracket so the center of the bracket aligns exactly with the center of the head track. Fasten the brackets in place with flathead screws.

Check the height of the doors in the opening, and trim if necessary. Insert pivot posts into predrilled holes at the bottoms and tops of the doors. Insert guide posts at the tops of the leading doors. Make sure all posts fit snugly.

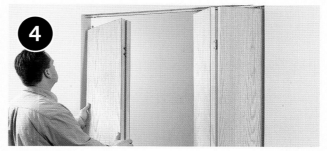

Fold one pair of doors closed and lift into position, inserting the pivot and guide posts into the head track. Slip the bottom pivot post into the anchor bracket. Repeat for the other pair of doors. Close the doors and check alignment along the side jambs and down the center. If necessary, adjust the top and bottom pivots following the manufacturer's instructions.

Installing Molding

The term *trim* refers to all of the moldings that dress up basement walls and ceilings, hide gaps and joints between surfaces, and adorn window and door frames. As a decorating tool, trim lends a sculptural quality to otherwise flat surfaces and can have a dramatic effect on any room in the house. Working with trim involves a few specific cuts and techniques, but once you learn them, you can install almost any type.

Crown molding decorates the intersection of walls and ceilings. Most crown molding is sprung, meaning it is installed at an angle to its nailing surfaces, leaving a hollow space behind it. It can be built up with several styles to create custom looks. In addition to wood, crown molding can be made with plastic polymers, often in ornate, one-piece styles.

Casing is trim that covers the edges of door and window jambs.

Picture rail is a traditional molding that installs parallel to crown molding and has a protruding rounded edge that holds hooks for hanging pictures. Similarly, a chair rail runs horizontally along walls, though at a height of 30 to 36 inches to serve as a border for wall-paper or wainscot, or as a transition between different paint colors. Both chair and picture rail are installed like baseboard.

Baseboard covers the bottoms of walls along the floor. Styles range from single-piece to built-up versions that include a base cap and a base shoe installed at the floor. Base shoe is small, typically rounded molding that is flexible and can follow contours in the floor to hide gaps left by the baseboard.

To avoid problems due to shrinkage after installation, stack the trim in the room where it will be installed and allow it to acclimate for several days. Apply a coat of primer or sealer to all sides of each piece, and let it dry thoroughly before installing it. You may also choose to paint or stain the trim before installing it.

Attach wood trim with finish nails, which have small heads that you drive below the surface using a nail set. Nails for most trim are size 6d or smaller, depending on the thickness of the trim and the wall surface. At a minimum, nails should be long enough to penetrate the framing by at least ¾"; heavier trim requires nails with more holding power. Use finish screws for securing trim to steel studs. After the trim is installed and all the nails are set, fill the nail holes with wood putty, and touch up the areas with paint or stain.

Trim moldings such as case molding and baseboard give a room a sense of completion.

How to Install Baseboard

Measure, cut, and install the first piece of baseboard. Butt both ends into the corners tightly. For longer lengths, it is a good idea to cut the piece slightly oversized (up to 1/16" on strips over 10 ft. long) and spring it into place. Nail the molding in place with two nails at every stud location.

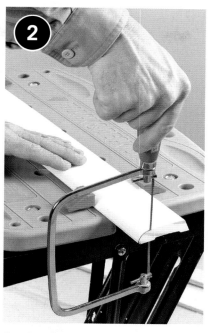

Cut the second piece of molding oversized by 6 to 10" and cope cut the adjoining end to the first piece. Fine-tune the cope with a metal file and sandpaper. Dry fit the joint, adjusting it as necessary to produce a tight-fitting joint.

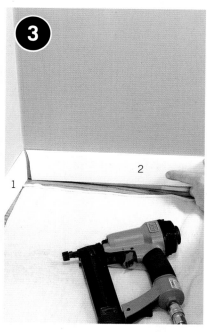

Make the inside corner joint. Use a T-bevel to transfer the proper angle. Cut the second piece (coped) to length and install it with two nails at each stud location.

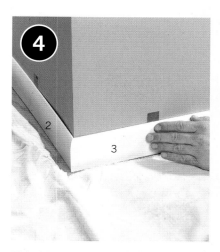

Make the outside corner joint. Test-fit the cut to ensure a tight joint (inset). Remove the mating piece of trim and fasten the first piece for the outside corner joint.

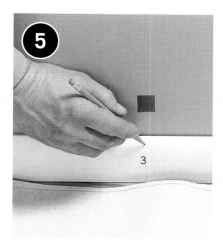

Lay out any scarf joints by placing the piece in position so that the previous joint is tight and then marking the center of a stud location nearest the opposite end. Set the angle of your saw to 30° and cut the molding at the marked location.

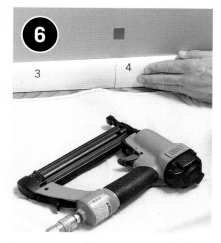

Nail the third piece in place, making sure the outside corner joint is tight. Cut the end of the fourth piece to match the scarf joint angle and nail it in place with two nails at each stud location. Add the remaining pieces of molding, fill the nail holes with putty, and apply a final coat of finish.

How to Install Door & Window Case Molding

TOOLS + MATERIALS

Case molding
Tape measure
Carpenter's pencil
Straightedge
Miter saw (or hand saw and miter box)
Drill and bits
Hammer
4d finish nails
Utility knife
Nail gun (optional)
Wood putty
Putty knife
Sandpaper
Paint, stain, or clear finish
Paintbrush
Work gloves
Safety glasses

On each jamb, mark a reveal line ⅛" from the inside edge. The casing will be installed flush with these lines. *Note: You can set the reveal at whatever dimension you choose, but make sure it's equal on all jambs.*

Place a length of casing along one side jamb, flush with the reveal line. At the top and bottom of the molding, mark the points where horizontal and vertical reveal lines meet. (When working with doors, mark the molding at the top only.)

Make 45° miter cuts on the ends of the moldings. Measure and cut the other vertical molding pieces using the same method.

Drill pilot holes spaced every 12" to prevent splitting, and attach the vertical casings with 4d finish nails driven through the casings and into the jambs. For doors, cut the side casings so the bottoms butt against the finished floor (bottom) or a plinth block.

 TIP

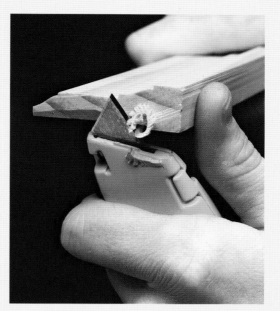

Back-cut the ends of casing pieces where needed using a sharp utility knife to help create tight joints.

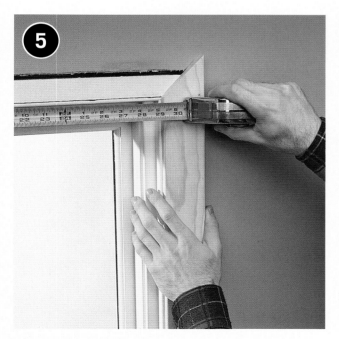

Measure the distance between the side casings, and cut top and bottom casings to fit with ends mitered at 45°. If the window or door unit is not perfectly square, make test cuts on scrap pieces to find the correct angle of the joints. Drill pilot holes and attach with finish nails.

Locknail the corner joints. Drill pilot holes and drive 4d finish nails through each corner, or drive finishing nails through each corner with a power nailer, as shown. If necessary, drive all nail heads below the wood surface using a nail set, then fill the nail holes with wood putty. Sand the puttied nail holes smooth and paint or stain the casings to match the rest of the trim in the room.

BASEMENT + GARAGE ROOM PROJECTS

Basement + Garage Room Projects

Creating a new room or rooms from scratch in a basement or garage requires some variations from how those rooms would be built in the main portion of the house. Fortunately, though, many of the specifics remain the same.

You can certainly choose the easiest option of simply finishing walls, ceilings, and floors so that you're left with one big multipurpose room. However, the most impressive basement and garage renovations work from a more well-defined plan that features a room or rooms with distinctive purposes. This chapter focuses on the details of creating those rooms. We have even included information on creating a fully featured "efficiency apartment" that could serve as stand-alone living quarter for family members, or even as a rental.

More likely, though, you'll have a particular use in mind. Whether it's a home gym, the ever-popular home theater (with true theater seating!), or just a family room for game night, you'll find what you need to know in this chapter.

In this chapter:
- Basement Bedroom
- Basement Bathroom
- Basement Kitchen
- Fun Family Room
- The Perfect Home Theater
- Laundry Center
- Quiet + Comfortable Home Office

A Basement Efficiency Apartment

The aging Baby Boomer generation, an unpredictable economy and record high real estate prices have all led to an increasing trend of multiple generations living under one roof. This is a case of turning back the clock to a time when families regularly shared living quarters and living expenses among parents, children and even grandchildren.

The apartment described in the pages that follow includes a nicely proportioned bedroom, a comfortable bathroom, and a modest kitchen.

Regardless of the floor plan you ultimately choose, an efficiency apartment such as this will likely require dealing with even more codes than you might in designing a part-time common area for the basement. Local fire and building codes strictly regulate basement living spaces, especially when it comes to crucial issues such as means of egress, the load on existing utilities, fire prevention, and universal design for the elderly or disabled.

UNIVERSAL DESIGN ELEMENTS

As the population ages, basement efficiency apartments are increasingly being designed to accommodate elderly parents, keeping them nearby. Ensuring the safety of elderly occupants—and making the space easier to use—means equipping the apartment with "universal design" elements, such as grab bars and lever door handles.

Attention-grabbing Grab Bars
Although the bars need to be positioned carefully and anchored correctly to wall studs to serve their purpose, you can choose from a wide range of designs. However, keep in mind cleanability when shopping for towel bars. Any mirrored finish such as polished chrome, stainless steel, or nickel will inevitably show fingerprints. Brushed versions of these materials will be easier to keep clean.

Bathing
A hand-held showerhead, whether used with a fixed showerhead or by itself, is key to a universal design bathroom. Bar showerheads are excellent choices, featuring a hand-held head positioned in a bracket that slides up and down a bar fixed to the shower wall.

If there is room for a bathtub in your basement bathroom, consider an accessibility tub. These feature high walls with a bench inside and a watertight door for easy access.

Handling Accessibility in Style
Lever handles are far easier for disabled or elderly people to use than knobs. Use lever handles on doors, sink faucets and bathroom faucets to make the whole apartment easier to use. Levers are also easier for small children to operate, and they can be amazingly stylish no matter where you use them.

As functional as they are, grab bars don't need to be dowdy. Today's selection includes finishes such as sleek polished chrome (left), and brushed nickel (right).

Lever-handled faucets are much easier for anyone with motor skill impairment or disabilities such as arthritis to use.

Hand-held showerheads such as this one provide flexibility for anyone with impaired mobility or weak grip strength. The rubberized handle, finger grips and overall design make this showerhead easy to hold and use even while water is blasting out of the showerhead.

Efficiency Apartment: Bedroom

A basement bedroom is the centerpiece of an efficiency apartment. This nicely sized room includes more than 140 square feet of living space, and a cedar-lined closet that will keep your clothes free from insects and smelling great. There is enough space in this bedroom to set up a reading area or small home office space, increasing the usefulness of the room.

However, any basement bedroom must have an egress window that meets minimum size and accessibility requirements (see page 27). A smoke detector is also required, and radon and carbon monoxide detectors are also smart additions to a basement room in which you'll be spending a lot of time. Although carpeting is usually not the best choice for basement flooring, it's a nice modest luxury in an efficiency apartment bedroom. Just take precautions in laying it so that no moisture gets trapped underneath.

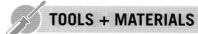

TOOLS + MATERIALS

Tape Measure	Multipurpose tool
Carpenter's pencil	Drill and bits
Level	Construction adhesive and caulk gun
Hammer	
Powder-actuated tool	Cedar paneling
2 × 4s or 2 × 6s	Drywall and drywall finishing tools
Egress window	Joint compound
Electrical cables, boxes, and wire nuts	Sanding paper

A closet is a very important part of any bedroom. As you'll see in the following pages, it is easy to build and equip. However, if you install a closet light, use one that stays cool.

How to Build a Basement Bedroom

Replace small basement windows with at least one egress window that is large enough to allow an adult to exit. Codes are absolutely clear that any inhabited room must have egress. Enlarge the window opening. Install a new window that meets code requirements for egress and install a code-compliant window well on the exterior side.

(continued)

Build all four stud walls, fastening sole plates to the concrete floor with a powder-actuated tool (see page 115). Walls built next to exterior walls should be stopped ½" short of the wall to prevent direct contact. Do not install vapor barriers.

Build the partition walls to frame the closet. Closets should be at least 32" deep from front to back. Walk-in closets are deeper. This closet will be equipped with a louvered bifold door, but it would also be a good place to install a pocket door.

Install light fixture boxes in the room's ceiling and closet. Consider what type of ceiling you'll be installing when positioning the fixtures. Recessed canister lights work well in a room. In closets, however, most codes require that only LED fluorescent or compact fluorescent bulbs are used because of the potential of incandescent bulbs to overheat in confined spaces.

Install the room wiring according to codes for minimum receptacle spacing and switch locations. Basement bedrooms do not require GFCI-protected receptacles, but they are a good idea nonetheless.

Add heating and cooling as needed. An electric baseboard heater is a common choice for basement rooms. Look for a model with a wall-mounted thermostat. While 120-volt heaters are available, 240-volt models are much more energy efficient. You will need to provide 240-volt service of course, usually in a 20-amp or 30-amp circuit, depending on the number of feet of heater you install.

Install mold-resistant wallboard on all walls, making sure the bottoms of the panels are at least ½" above the floor. Do not insulate exterior walls. You may insulate interior walls for soundproofing. Use unfaced fiberglass. *Note: Have preliminary wiring inspections done before closing up walls.*

Line the closet walls. Here aromatic cedar paneling is being installed on the closet interior, and standard mold-resistant wallboard is going onto the room side of the walls. Cedar is naturally resistant to moisture-related rot.

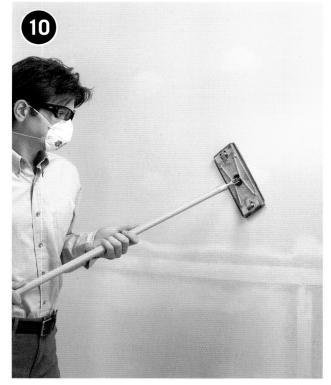

Finish the walls by taping seams and covering tape and screwheads with joint compound. Apply a coat of primer and then paint.

(continued)

Install the remaining electrical fixtures and make wiring hookups. The electric baseboard heater being installed here is sited beneath the window because that is the most efficient location for a heater. Have final electrical inspections performed. Install the ceiling of your choice.

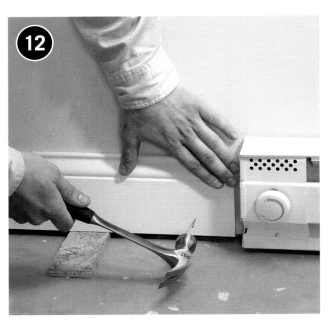

Install trim, including baseboard trim and window and door trim. Maintain a gap of at least ½" between base trim and baseboard heaters. Prepaint or stain the trim pieces before installation for a neater job. Egress windows can be trimmed with custom jambs and casing.

Install closet shelves. Closet organizers made from vinyl-coated wire are good choices for basements because they allow maximum air circulation and will not contribute to mold or mildew problems.

Install the closet door. A bifold door with louvers is a good choice for basement bedroom closets because it allows ventilation. Louvers can be time-consuming to paint, however. Install the floor coverings of your choice.

The Basement Suite Bathroom

A bathroom is an essential addition to any basement efficiency apartment because it is key to making the suite as useful and independent of the upstairs space as possible. Of course, bathrooms are wonderful basement additions, regardless of what other types of rooms you may be adding.

Many new homes are plumbed with basement stub-outs in place. More likely, you'll need to break up the concrete floor to install a new drain and supply plumbing. With a jackhammer and some help, this is a manageable DIY project.

Because plastic pipes cannot be encased in concrete, they must be laid in granular fill beneath the basement floor. Potential locations for your bathroom are therefore limited by how close the main sewer line is to the floor service where it meets the main drain stack. Check local codes for other restrictions in your area.

Once you've cut into the main waste vent, there can be no drainage in the house until you have fully installed the new branch lines and sealed the joints. Have extra pipe and fittings on hand. Cutting through concrete produces lots of dust. Block off other areas of the basement with plastic sheeting, and wear an approved dust mask or respirator.

A half bath or three-quarter bath like this one can turn a basement into a livable addition and is the heart and soul of a basement efficiency apartment. It is also, of course, a wonderful addition to any basement design.

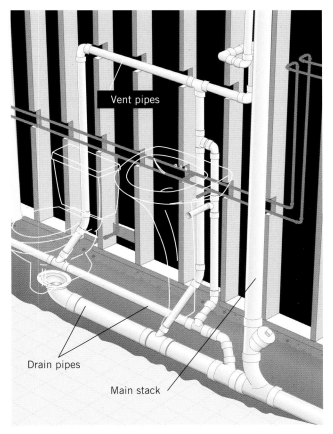

Vent pipes

Drain pipes

Main stack

Our demonstration bathroom includes a shower, toilet, and pedestal sink arranged in a line to simplify trenching. A 2" drainpipe services the new shower and sink; a 3" pipe services the new toilet. The drainpipes converge at a Y-fitting joined to the existing main drain. The toilet and sink have individual vent pipes that meet inside the wet wall before extending up into the attic, where they join the main waste-vent stack.

How to Plumb a Basement Bath

Mark the proposed location of the bathroom on the basement floor using tape. Include the walls, wet wall, and fixture locations. The easiest configuration is to install all the fixtures against the wet wall, which will contain the water supply and vents. The drain lines should run parallel to the wet wall in the most direct route to the main waste-vent stack. Mark the drain line location (typically around 6" out from the wet wall).

Enclose the work area with plastic sheeting to protect the rest of the house. Cut out the area around the main stack. Use a concrete saw or a circular saw with a masonry blade to score a 24 × 24" square cutting line around the waste-vent stack. The cut should be at least 1" deep.

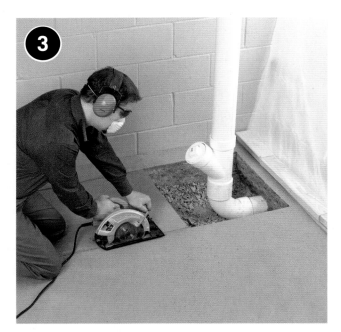

Use a cold chisel and hand maul to strike along scored cut lines and chip out concrete around the main soil stack. Take care not to damage the pipe. Determine the depth of the sewer line where it meets the main stack. Use a chalk line to outline a 24"-wide trench over the new branch line. Score the lines with a circular saw fit with masonry blade.

Use a jackhammer to break up the concrete in the trench, taking care not to damage any of the existing plumbing lines. Wear gloves, eye and ear protection, and a dust mask. Remove the concrete for disposal. Remove dirt from the trench, starting at the main waste-vent stack.

5

1" spacer

Create a flat-bottomed trench that slopes toward the main stack at ¼" per ft. The soil will hold up the drain lines, so it is important to create an even surface. Use a hand tamper to tamp down the soil if it has been disturbed. Tape a 1" spacer to the end of a 4-ft. level to create a handy measuring tool for checking the proper slope. Set the soil aside to use for backfill.

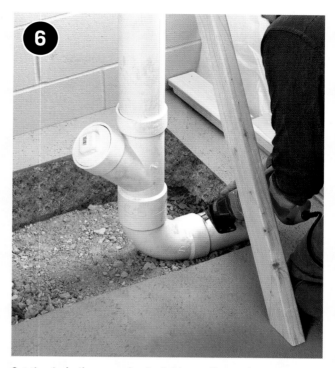

6

Cut the drain line or main stack (depending on how deep the drain line is) using a reciprocating saw (or a snap cutter). Support the main waste-vent stack before cutting. Use a 2 × 4 and duct tape for a plastic stack, or riser clamps for a cast-iron stack. If cutting the horizontal drain line, cut as close as possible to the stack.

7

Cleanout

Cut into the stack above the cleanout, and remove the pipe and fittings. Wear rubber gloves, and have a large plastic bag and rags ready, as old pipes and fittings may be coated with sewer sludge. Remember that no wastewater can flow in the house while the pipes are cut open. Turn off the water and drain toilets to prevent accidental use.

(continued)

CAST IRON WASTE STACKS

Depending on the age of your home, your vertical waste stack may be cast iron. Cutting an iron stack requires a different approach than shown here. You'll need to use a snap cutter, available from most large rental centers. Be absolutely sure you know how to use the cutter, because improper use can lead to injury and damage the waste stack. If you aren't confident using a snap cutter, you can hire a plumber to execute just this step of the project. You can use special fittings to tie a PVC drain line into a cast iron waste stack.

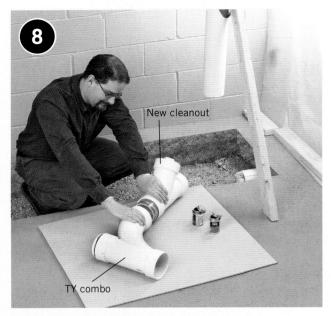

Cut and test fit a new cleanout and long sweep TY combo assembly, dry-fitting it to the drain stack and the horizontal drain line to the street. Make any needed adjustments and then solvent-glue the fittings and new pipe into a single assembly.

Clean the outside of the old pipes thoroughly and apply primer. Also apply primer and solvent glue to the female surfaces of the union fittings in the assembly. Slide the fitting assembly over the primed ends of the drain stack and the drain line at the same time. This requires a little bit of play in one or both of the lines so you can manipulate the new assembly. If your existing pipes will not move at all, you'll need to use a banded coupling on the drain stack to seal the gap.

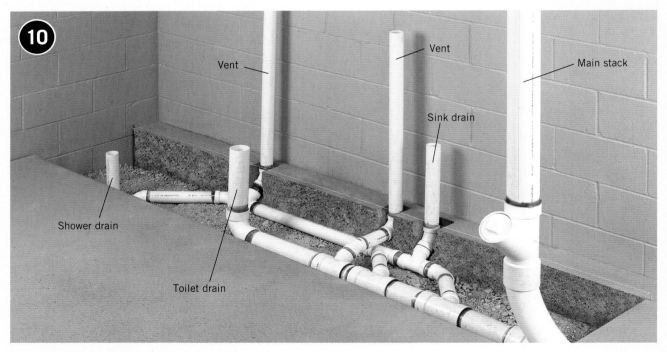

Cut and fit the components of the new drain line one piece at a time, starting at the stack. Use strings or boards to outline the wet wall, so vent placement is correct. Drain lines underground must be a minimum of 2". Use 3 × 2" reducing Ys to tie the shower drain line and the sink drain line into the toilet drain line. Install vertical drain and vent lines that are long enough to protrude well above the level of the finished floor.

Check for leaks by pouring water into each new drainpipe. If the joints appear sound, contact your building department and arrange for your inspection (you must do this prior to covering the pipes). Plug the pipe openings with rags to prevent sewer gas from escaping. *Note: Some municipalities require an air test as well.*

Backfill around the pipes with the soil dug from the trench. Mix and pour new concrete to cover the trench, and trowel smooth. Allow the concrete to cure for three days. Some municipalities may require that isolation membrane be wrapped around vertical pipes where they will be surrounded by concrete—check with your local inspector.

Build the wet wall from 2 × 6 lumber. The sill plate should be pressure treated, but the other members may be SPF. Notch the sill plate so the vent pipes clear it easily. Use masonry anchors or concrete nails and a powder-actuated nailer to attach the plate.

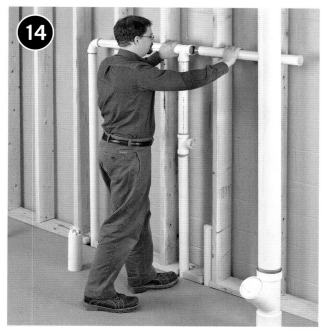

Run 2" vent pipes through notches in the studs. Assemble with vent T and 90° fittings. The 2" pipes are larger than required, but using the same size as the drain lines eliminates the need for reducing fittings and makes for less waste. The 90° fittings are typically less expensive than the vent elbows.

(continued)

Route the vent pipe to a point beneath a wall cavity running from the basement to the attic. Or, if there is another vent line closer that you can tie into, go ahead and do that.

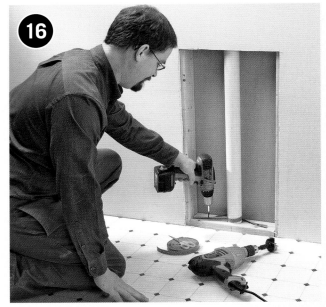

Run vent pipe up through the floors above and either directly out through the roof or tie it to another vent pipe in the attic. Remove sections of wall surface as needed to bore holes for running the vent pipe through wall plates. Feed the vent pipe up into the wall cavity from the basement. Wedge the vent pipe in place while you solvent-glue the fittings. Support the vent pipe at each floor with plastic pipe hangers installed horizontally. Stuff fiberglass insulation into holes around pipes. Do not replace any wall coverings until you have had your final inspection.

Nail guard

Install the water supply plumbing. Compared to the drain-vent plumbing, this will seem remarkably easy. Although the copper supply pipes shown here are still common in home applications, many plumbers and homeowners are opting for the easier and quicker option of PEX supply pipes and fittings.

SOLDERING

Use caution when soldering copper. Pipes and fittings become very hot and must be allowed to cool before handling.

How to Build a Basement or Garage Bathroom

Frame the new walls using pressure-treated sole plates. If walls will contain additional plumbing, build them from 2 × 6 stock.

Install framing for the bathroom door (see pages 128 to 129). For economy, a 30"-wide prehung interior door makes sense, but if you want to conserve space consider installing a pocket door. They are fairly common for bathroom applications.

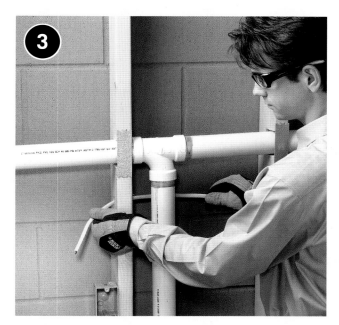

Install 12/2 NM sheathed cable to supply power for a dedicated 20-amp small appliance circuit. Most codes have specific requirements for spacing. The circuit must have GFCI protection. You can wire it with individually protected GFCI receptacles or install a 20-amp GFCI breaker in the main service panel. If you do not have experience with home wiring, hire a professional.

Wire ceiling lights and any wall lights for a lighted medicine chest. Recessed canister lights are a good choice for basements because they don't project down into the room. (Be sure the fixtures you're installing are damp rated for bathroom use.) Have all wiring inspected and approved before you close up the walls.

(continued)

Add ventilation. Basement vents require powered vent fans that can be wall-mounted or ceiling mounted. The ductwork for the fan exhaust is normally routed out through a hole in the rim joist of the house. If the bathroom contains a shower or bathtub, the duct must terminate outdoors. If it is only a half bath some codes allow you to vent into an attic.

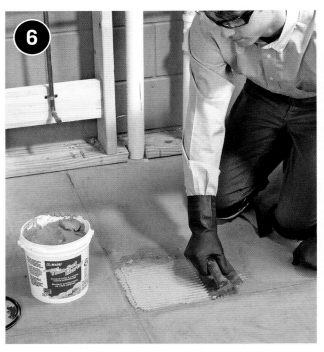

Install floor coverings. Here a bed of thinset mortar is being laid for textured porcelain floor tiles. The mortar bed usually can be applied directly to the concrete floor.

Trim floor covering materials to fit around drainpipes in the floor, such as the toilet drain stub-out seen here. Complete the floor covering installation.

Install the shower pan according to the manufacturer's instructions. Some are set into a bed of mortar or mastic while others are fastened to the wall framing. Trim the drainpipe to the recommended height first (bottom photo) and make all drain connections.

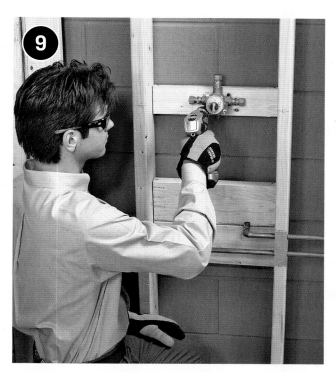

Install shower supply pipes and make hookups to the faucet body. *Note: The easiest shower stalls to install are freestanding, but kits and tileboard units that are installed in framed alcoves are cheaper. Read the directions that come with your stall to see if they recommend installing panels, such as cementboard, as backer before you install the shower.*

Install the shower enclosure kit or make your custom shower surround with tileboard.

Install ceiling coverings. While there are advantages to installing a suspended ceiling or acoustic tile ceiling that's easy to remove for access, mold-resistant wallboard is economical, paintable, and has a finished room feel that the other types lack.

Install wall coverings. Do not use standard wallboard. Use mold-resistant wallboard or cementboard throughout. Do not install a vapor barrier behind the wallboard.

(continued)

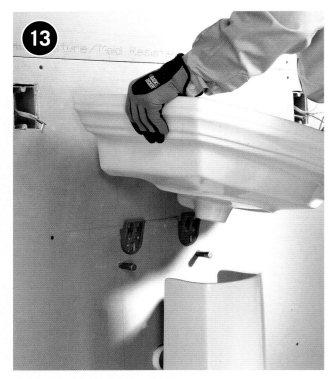

Attach any other wall-mounted fixtures, such as the pedestal sink being hung on a mounting plate above. Do all of the work requiring access to wall or ceiling stud cavities before you install the wall coverings. And don't neglect to have inspections done.

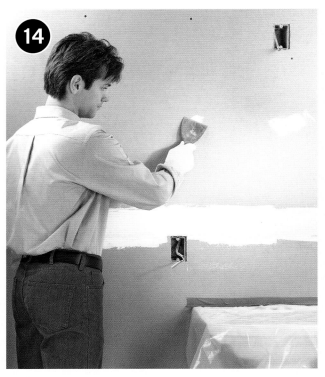

Cover seams and fill holes in the walls and ceiling with fiberglass wallboard tape and joint compound. Sand the compound smooth and apply a coat of wallboard primer.

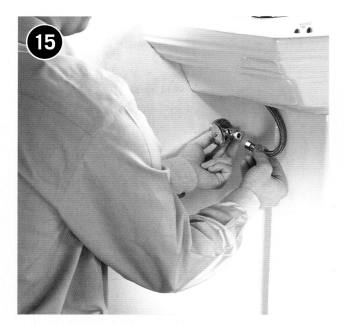

Finish making the supply and drain hookups for the lavatory. Add faucets to all fixtures and test them.

Install the toilet after trimming the closet drain pipe to the correct height. Hook up the water supply to the fill valve and then test the operation. Drain times can be a bit slower in basements, and flushes may be weakened slightly by the shallowness of the drain line slopes.

17

Paint the walls and ceiling using a paint with a mold-resistant additive. Paint the ceiling first. For bathrooms, choose a washable, semigloss paint.

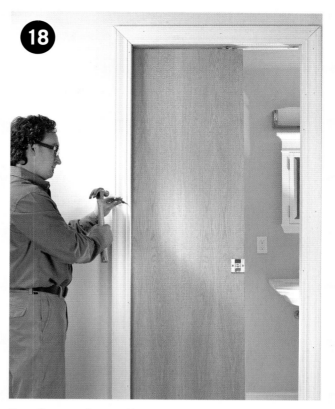

18

Hang the entry door and install trim around the door as well as a baseboard trim. You may find it easier to paint or finish the door and trim before installation.

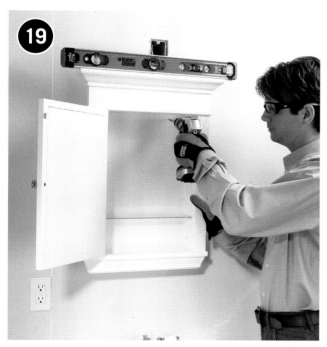

19

Install mirrors, medicine cabinets, towel rods, paper holders, and any other members of the decorative bathroom suite.

20

Attach trim kits and escutcheons to light fixtures and vent fans. Add switch plates and receptacle covers, too. Test all fixtures.

Basement or Garage Kitchen

A small kitchen or kitchenette can make or break an efficiency apartment, and it's also a wonderful complement to any other room you might be building in the basement or garage, from a big game room where snacks will be the order of the day, to a home theater that can become a dinner theater with the help of some quick cooking.

However, this kitchen is ideally suited for an efficiency apartment where it can piggyback off the changes you'll already be making to the space to accommodate the function of the bathroom. The most common efficiency kitchen is an "L" design, with the sink on one wall and the range and stove on a perpendicular wall. If only one wall is available given space constraints, use a straight-run galley kitchen design.

Refer to the steps already outlined in the bathroom project for instruction on how to tie in the kitchen sink's drain and water supply lines. It's generally best to keep plumbing to a minimum; the more sluggish drainage in this part of the house usually prohibits the inclusion of a garbage disposal or washer. You can make plumbing this room easier by using PEX pipe and fixtures.

You'll also need to accommodate the added electrical burden, especially if you choose an electrical range like the one in this project. See more information about upgrading your electrical system and running a new circuit on pages 56 to 65. An electric range is usually the easiest option, although if you happen to have gas line stub-outs in place in the basement, you can opt for a gas range and oven (but have a professional make the gas connections).

The design here includes a half-height refrigerator, which usually serves the more modest needs of a basement apartment. You can upgrade to a full-size unit for a reasonable additional expense. In either case, a full-function kitchen completes an efficiency apartment, making it truly self-sufficient. Introduce a few appliances, the essential utensils, pots and pans and other cookware, and there's no meal you can't make in this streamlined room.

A straight-run galley kitchen such as this is an efficient layout for a basement kitchen, and it's simple to build, as well. Using shelves in place of some cabinets saves money and is a handy type of storage.

AN EFFICIENCY KITCHEN

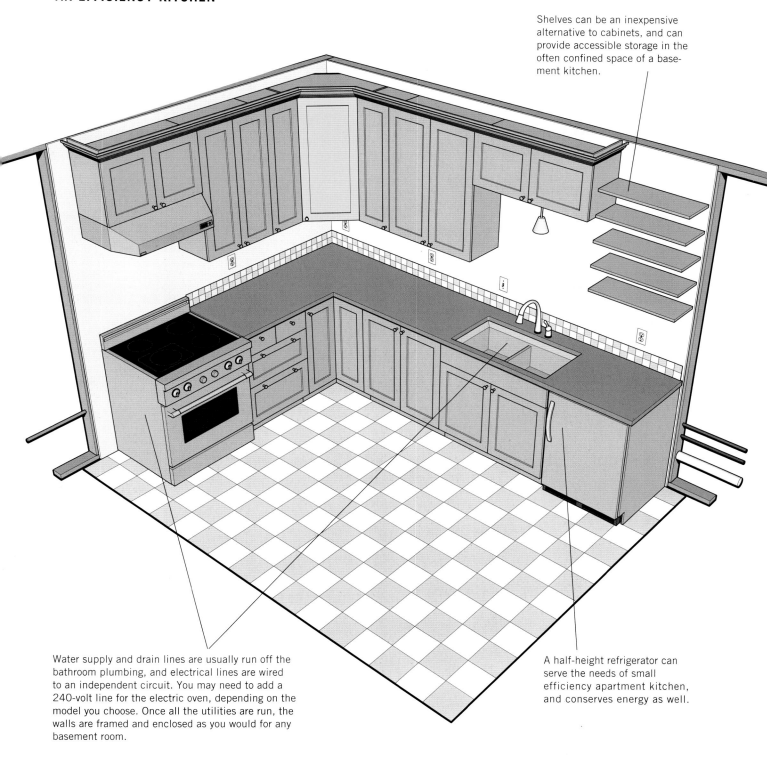

Shelves can be an inexpensive alternative to cabinets, and can provide accessible storage in the often confined space of a basement kitchen.

Water supply and drain lines are usually run off the bathroom plumbing, and electrical lines are wired to an independent circuit. You may need to add a 240-volt line for the electric oven, depending on the model you choose. Once all the utilities are run, the walls are framed and enclosed as you would for any basement room.

A half-height refrigerator can serve the needs of small efficiency apartment kitchen, and conserves energy as well.

A basic "L" kitchen such as this is a space-conserving space that is easy to work in and perfectly suited to many different basement configurations.

How to Install Efficiency Kitchen Cabinets

Mark the walls for cabinet placement by measuring up 34½" from the level floor surface, and marking a reference line (use a level to do this—a laser level works best). Base cabinets will be installed with top edges flush against this line. Measure up 84" from the floor and draw a second reference line. Wall cabinets will be installed with their top edges flush against this line.

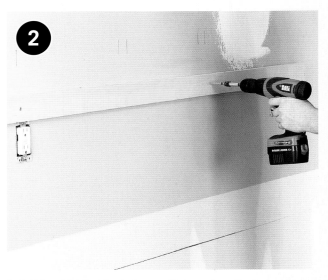

Install 1 × 3 temporary ledgers with top edges flush against the reference lines. This basement had preexisting wall board on the top half of the walls, so the ledger will be marked with stud location. If you've installed new walls, you don't need to mark the ledger. Cabinets will rest temporarily on ledgers during installation (the ledgers alone will not support them, however).

Position the corner upper cabinet first, making sure it is resting cleanly on the ledger. Drill ³⁄₁₆" pilot holes into the wall studs through the hanging strips at the top rear of the cabinet. Attach the cabinet to the wall with 2½" screws. Do not tighten fully until all cabinets are hung.

Attach a filler strip to the front edge of the cabinet, if needed. Clamp it in place, drill counterbored pilot holes through the cabinet near hinge locations, and screw filler to cabinet. Position the adjoining cabinet on the ledger, tight against the corner cabinet or filler strip. Clamp in place, top and bottom. Check the front edges for plumb. Drill ³⁄₁₆" pilot holes into the wall studs through the hanging strips in the rear of the cabinet and screw the cabinet to the wall. Don't tighten the screws fully until all the cabinets are hung.

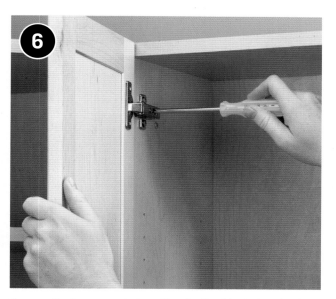

Continue installing cabinets next to installed cabinets. Join the cabinets with the screws supplied or as directed by the manufacturer. Fill gaps between cabinets or cabinet and wall with filler strips.

Remove the temporary ledger. Check all cabinets for plumb and tighten the wall screws completely. Cut off exposed shims with a utility knife. Cover gaps with trim moldings and install the cabinet doors. If necessary, adjust the hinges so that the doors are straight and plumb.

 FACE-FRAME VS. FRAMELESS

Face-frame cabinets include frames around the front of the cabinet box. The door opening space is reduced and a certain amount of "dead" space exists within the cabinet behind the frames. Hinges mount on the frame. The door itself may be flush within the frame or raised above it. This is a more traditional look.

Frameless cabinets are often referred to as "European style." They have no face-frame and doors and drawers span the entire width of the carcass, which allows easier access and a bit more storage space. The doors are mounted using cup hinges that are invisible when the doors are closed. Frameless cabinets are a streamlined contemporary look. One drawback is that the cabinets do not have the added strength of the face frame, so it is critical that they are solidly constructed and properly installed.

Installing Efficiency Kitchen Base Cabinets

Place the corner cabinet first, checking for plumb and level. If necessary, drive wood shims under any cabinet to level it. Drill pilot holes and screw the cabinet to the wall with wood screws. Clamp an adjoining cabinet to the corner cabinet and follow the same leveling and attachment process. Drill counterbored pilot holes through the cabinet sides and screw the cabinets together.

Make sure all the cabinets are level. If necessary, adjust by driving shims under the base of the cabinets. Place the shims behind the cabinets near the stud locations to fill any gaps. Tighten the wall screws. Cut off the shims with a utility knife.

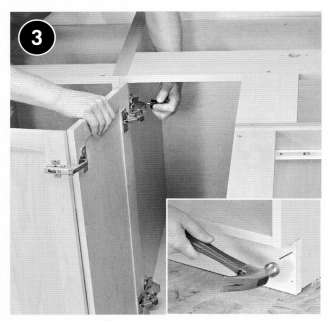

Use trim moldings to cover gaps between the cabinets and the wall or floor. Install toe-kick molding if supplied (inset). Hang cabinet doors and mount the drawer fronts, then test to make sure they close smoothly and the doors fit evenly and flush. Self-closing cabinet hinges (by far the most common type installed today) have adjustment screws that allow you to make minor adjustments.

FREESTANDING BASE CABINETS

Freestanding kitchen cabinets have become a popular option, especially for base cabinets (matched top cabinets are usually offered with the base cabinets). They offer portability and interchangeability (sink base cabinets being a notable exception). These cabinets are sold ready to assemble and installation is similar to attached cabinets but most styles are self-leveling (you adjust the feet or legs). A freestanding cabinet island or sink base cabinet must be secured in place to prevent movement.

Installing Efficiency Kitchen Countertops

  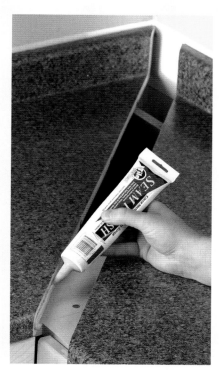

One of the least expensive options for a basement kitchen counter is the post-form type shown here. It is a simple job to mark and cut sink cutouts and edges with a jigsaw. The countertop is held in place at seams, end caps and on cabinet top edges with a bead of silicone caulk. Joints are held together from underneath with miter take-up bolts.

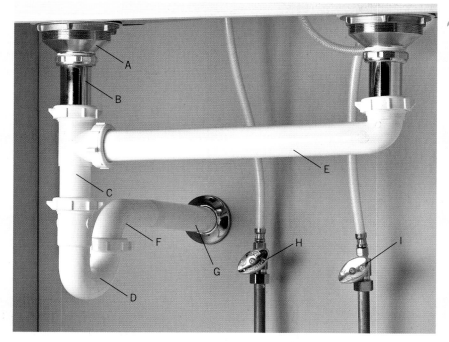

Because of the lack of extra appliances such as dishwashers, basic basement kitchen sink plumbing usually involves the simple set-up shown here (this includes a sink with two bowls). Strainer basket (A), tailpiece (B), continuous waster T (C), P- or S-trap (D), outlet drain lines (E), trap arm (F), wall stubout (G), hot supply (H), and cold supply (I).

 TIP

Local codes governing kitchen ventilation vary widely from municipality, ranging from many codes that don't regulate the issue at all, to a few that don't allow ductless (self-venting) range hoods. Check with your local building authorities; in most cases you will not be required to install a range vent hood. However, if you planning on regularly cooking in the kitchenette you've installed, a range hood can help eliminate odors and limit smoke in the space. You can find inexpensive plug-in range hoods with cleanable filters that would be fine for the small range included in this project.

This cozy family room features a vent-free gas fireplace and a brand new patio door that opens out to a lower level walkout patio.

A Basement or Garage Family Room

Many homeowners are hesitant to commit a basement or garage renovation to a single purpose-driven room or suite. A family room project is a great way to straddle that fence. The room can be a quiet, contemplative refuge at one moment, and then serve as a gathering place for the family on special occasions. Family rooms can also easily transform into a home gym, yoga studio, billiards and ping pong arcade, crafts center, or a combination.

The project in this section includes a fireplace. This is an amazingly popular addition for basement renovations across the country, but could also serve a garage renovation extremely well—especially if the home's living room does not have one. As you'll discover, installing a fireplace is often easier than a DIY homeowner might imagine. It's made even easier with the rise of "ventless" units that alleviate the need to duct smoke out through an exterior wall.

Manufacturers offer fireplaces in a vast range of styles, from traditional fireboxes to sleek, modern, flush-fitting units with LED-lit log beds. Regardless of the type, though, a fireplace provides dry heat to spaces that are often a bit humid and chilly.

One important caveat though: It is essential to consult your local building department to not only make sure the fireplace is code compliant, but also to guarantee the installation is safe for the whole family.

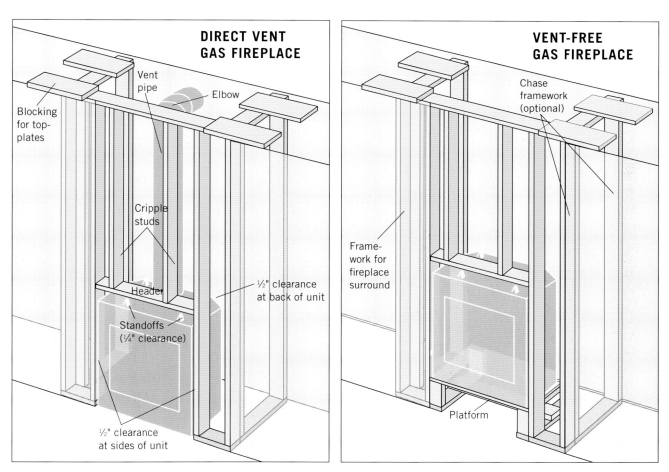

Gas fireplaces come in two types for home use: direct vent (left), which must be exhausted to the home exterior, and vent-free, which do not require venting but must be installed in either an existing firebox or a specially designed firebox that circulates air and exhaust internally. Vent-free models are allowed in Canada and several American states. Check with your local zoning or building department.

How to Build a Family Room with Fireplace

Frame the new walls for the room. Here, an open area in a walkout basement with a finished exterior wall is being divided into a smaller finished space for a family room with direct access to a patio.

Install wiring cables in the stud walls). Because family rooms normally include several types of electronic devices, consider adding multimedia outlets for coaxial cable and speaker cables.

Install fixture boxes for lights keeping the planned ceiling material thickness and installation method in mind. Here, a box is being installed for a 6-ft. section of halogen track lighting to provide adjustable lighting that can be focused on the fireplace mantel.

Frame the opening for the firebox according to the manufacturer's directions and minimum clearances. Because the fireplace surround planned for this room uses 12 × 12" wall tile around the opening, we added full-height studs so the required cementboard backer can be seamed with the wallboard over a stud. A header for the opening is supported by short jack studs at the sides.

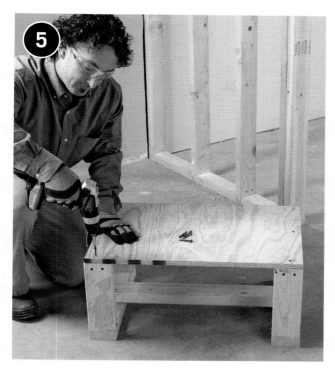

Construct a support platform for the firebox. Because the firebox will be housed in open space on the other side of the fireplace wall, we were able to get by with a simple wood platform built with 2 × 4s and ¾" plywood.

Secure the firebox platform in the wall opening by nailing or screwing it to the studs at the edges of the opening. Some manufacturers may require that you secure the platform to the floor as well.

Install wallboard on ceiling. When wallboarding both the ceiling and the walls, it is usually recommended that you do the ceiling first so the vertical panels can be butted up against the ceiling to provide some extra support. If you are hanging a suspended or tile ceiling, wallboard the walls first.

Cut cementboard into strips equal in width to the dimension of your tiled surround and attach them to the 2 × 4 nailers bordering the framed firebox opening. It is generally a good idea to predrill for cementboard screws, especially with narrower strips.

(continued)

Install mold-resistant wallboard in the rest of the room, keeping the bottom edges at least ½" above the floor. If you have planned your firebox framing properly, all wallboard edges will fall over studs or cross blocks.

Apply joint compound and fiberglass seam tape over seams and cover screwheads with compound. Sand the compound smooth.

Prime and paint the ceiling and the walls. To boost the visual interest of the ceiling, we added some texture to the ceiling paint (above) and applied it with a ⅝" nap roller. The effect is much subtler than the iconic, and often asbestos-containing, cottage cheese ceiling of the 1960s and '70s.

Apply a mortar bed for the tile surround using a notched trowel (a ¼" square-notch trowel is typical but check the recommendations on the thinset package label). Apply only as much mortar as you can tile in about 10 minutes. Treating each leg of the square surround separately is a good strategy.

Press the surround tiles into the mortar bed and set them by pressing with a short piece of 2 × 4 wrapped in a soft cloth. Most tiles have spacing nubs cast into the edges so setting the gaps between tiles or tile sheets is automatic. If your tiles do not have spacing nubs, use plastic tile spacers available at your tile store. Let the thinset mortar dry overnight once you're finished setting the tiles.

Apply dark-tinted grout to the tiles using a grout float. Let the grout harden slightly and then buff off the residue with a soft, clean cloth.

Begin adding surround trim. Here, 1 × 4 cherry casing is being attached to wall stud locations. The side casings should be slightly off the floor (if you have not installed flooring yet account for the floor covering thickness) and butted against the tile surround. If you have planned properly, there will be wall studs behind the casing. *Note: We chose 1 × 4 cherry because it is attractive, but also because you can usually buy it dimensioned, planed, and sanded on all sides at the lumber yard. If you have woodworking equipment, use any lumber you like.*

Add built-up head casing. The head casing should overhang the side casings by an inch or so. We used a built-up technique to add some depth and profile to the head casing. First attach a full-width 1 × 4 to the wall. Then, install a 1 × 3 so the ends and top are flush with the ends and top of the 1 × 4. Finally, install a cherry 1 × 2 in the same manner.

(continued)

Cut and install the mantel board. We used another piece of 1 × 4 cherry the same length as the head casings, but if you have access to woodworking tools consider a thicker board for a little more presence. Or, face-glue two 1 × 4s together.

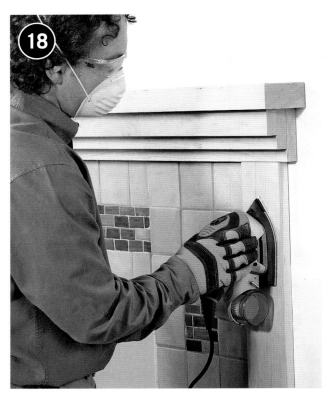

Finish-sand all the cherry and then apply a light wood stain. After the stain dries, topcoat with a cherry-tone or light mahogany wipe-on varnish that will even out the uneven coloration typical with cherry. Fill nail holes with cherry-tinted wood putty.

Set the firebox for the fireplace into the finished surround and check for level. Fasten it to the framing by nailing or screwing through the nailing flange, depending on the manufacturer's recommendations.

Seal the gap around the firebox with high-temperature silicone sealant. Do not use ordinary caulk here because it could melt or even catch fire.

Run natural gas supply pipe to within 18" or so of the gas inlet port on the side of the firebox. Attach a stop cock to the supply tube. *Warning: Working with gas pipe and making gas hookups is very dangerous and in many municipalities it may only be done by a licensed professional. Doing the work yourself may also void the warranty on your gas appliance. It is strongly recommended that you hire a professional for this part of the project.*

Connect the fireplace to the gas supply with a flexible gas connector tube, making sure to use gas-rated teflon tape to lubricate screw threads on the connector. Restore the gas supply and test all connections with leak detector spray (inset).

Install floor coverings. Snap-together laminate planks are easy to install and in general a good choice for basement family rooms. Trim the laminate planks to fit around the fireplace casings.

Install baseboard moldings, lighting trim kits, and any other finishing trim such as door casings. Remember to read the vent-free fireplace manual thoroughly and follow all safety precautions for operation. Have the unit inspected annually to make sure it is still operating properly.

Today's technology offers homeowners the opportunity to create a one-of-a-kind basement theater that will put commercial theaters to shame. This stunning space features an 85-inch screen, upscale textured acoustic panels that stop echoes and prevent the theater's sound system from bothering occupants in the rest of the house, custom seating with a carpeted riser, and even adjustable lighting for the optimal viewing experience. You may not be able to go this far in your own basement, but you can certainly have a spectacular theater experience without breaking the bank.

A Basement or Garage Home Theater

Gone are the days of a gigantic, bulky TV on a console at one end of a family room or living room. Modern TVs are flat, sleek, and more sophisticated than ever before. Technology has also evolved to create jaw-dropping colors, sharpness, and motion handling. Taking advantage of all those features to create the ultimate home-theater experience usually means mounting the TV on a wall.

THE VIEW

A TV purchase is no longer just a matter of screen size, your favorite brand, and the cost. Now you can choose from mini-LED, ULED, QLED, OLED, and more. To make matters more confusing, each manufacturer uses different proprietary terms to describe what are essentially common specifications and features.

Screen height. Regardless of size or technology, the height at which the TV is placed will have a dramatic effect on how comfortable it is to watch. This is where homeowners most often get it wrong. The center of the TV screen should be level with the viewer's eyes. Start with how you view the TV.

If you usually watch while seated on a couch, measure from the floor to your eyes. However, if you more commonly view the TV all the way back in a recliner, the viewing angle may be several inches lower. These measurements should guide where you wall-mount the TV, or the height of the TV stand or console you use under a TV that's not wall mounted.

Viewing distance. This crucial factor will be affected by the TV, the room dimensions, furniture positioning, and your own preferences. Most recommendations call for sitting closer than the average viewer would find comfortable. That's because today's TVs offer a far more detailed picture than models even a decade ago. However, modern TVs are also generally brighter, and can lead to eye strain if you sit too close. See the chart below for commonsense recommendations—and consult the manufacturer's guidance—but adjust the distance to what is most comfortable for your eyes.

You'll notice that the recommended distance is less for viewing on an angle. That's because the image on a modern flat-panel TV technology is generally poorer than the same image viewed straight on. This too is subject to variation, depending on the TV and its native technology. Experimentation will be your best friend in setting up your own basement or garage theater.

Lighting. This is another area of common misunderstanding. Although we think of a cinema experience as a brightly lit screen in a totally dark room, that's incorrect. The image will be most attractive to your eyes—and less likely to strain them—with side lighting (as long it doesn't reflect on the screen or create a hot-spot glare). It's wise to plan for subtle LED lighting behind the TV panel itself, diffuse lighting behind and to the side of viewers, or both. The ideal basement home theater viewing environment is neither totally dark nor brightly lit.

 RECOMMENDED VIEWING DISTANCES BY TV SIZE

The recommendations here include minimum and maximum distances, that actually relate to field of view (FOV), expressed in the viewing angle. The closer you are, the wider the FOV and the more difficult it will be to take in the entire scene on the screen. The maximum distance will normally provide a more enjoyable viewing experience, and lower risk of eye strain. Cinema professionals recommend a viewing angle of around 30 percent.

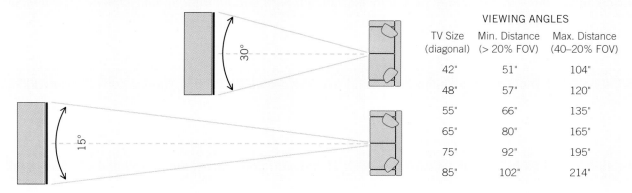

	VIEWING ANGLES	
TV Size (diagonal)	Min. Distance (> 20% FOV)	Max. Distance (40–20% FOV)
42"	51"	104"
48"	57"	120"
55"	66"	135"
65"	80"	165"
75"	92"	195"
85"	102"	214"

A Custom Home Theater Riser

This platform has been designed to be easy to build, sturdy, and soundproof. Once completed, it creates a luxurious theater experience with all the comforts of home.

You may need nothing more than a comfy couch or a couple of recliners if you've created a modest basement or garage home theater to watch the occasional streamed movie or your favorite TV sitcoms. There is nothing wrong with a smaller, less ambitious home theater.

But if you're after something closer to a true cinema experience for watching newly released movies with a group of friends—or regularly have a crowd of college buddies over to watch sports in comfort that's second only to 50-yard-line seats, you'll want to add a seating riser to the room.

Risers are platforms that create true theater or stadium seating, in progressively elevated rows. They are ideal for home theaters that regularly host large groups to watch movies on a large TV. A riser allows everyone in the party to have a clear view of the screen while sitting in the height of comfort.

The riser in this project is simple and does not require advanced woodworking or construction skills. The most important requirement is a focus on details to get the measurements exactly right. Beyond that, you'll need a few basic tools that you probably already own. This project was designed for a particular space butted to a back wall and sandwiched between two side walls. That creates a custom look the fits perfectly with the room. Adding to the look, this riser has a built-in step.

You can and should adapt this design to the dimensions of your own basement or garage home theater. However, we suggest maintaining the platform depth described here because it was intentionally designed to accommodate typical recliner measurements—which allow for reclining without hitting the chair headrest against the back wall or the footrest against the seating in the lower row. Check local building codes for other restrictions related to headroom; if your basement ceiling is particularly low, a riser may not be advisable or even allowed.

If, on the other hand, the basement ceilings are particularly high (or you're building the theater in a garage), you can consider adding an additional riser for a third row of seats.

You'll notice that this platform includes rock wool insulation. This isn't used to prevent heat or cold transfer, but is rather for its sound-dampening properties. The last thing you want in a home theater are annoying creaks whenever someone on the top row moves around.

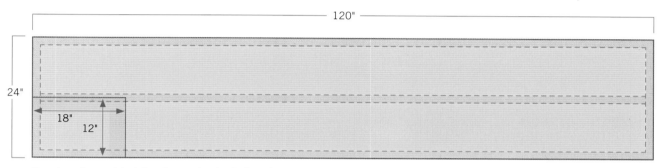

Top view of completed riser frame showing bottom frame elements.

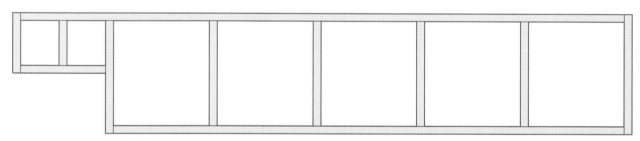

Top view of top frame.

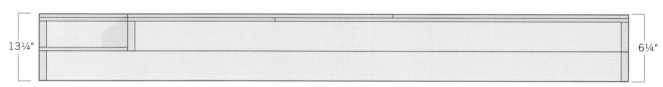

Side view of finished riser frame.

How to Build a Home Theater Riser

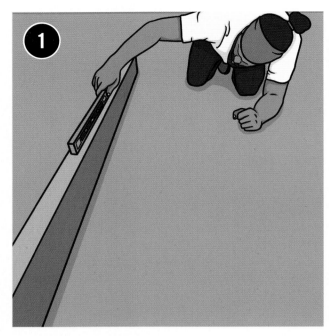

Clean the floor thoroughly. Use a long straight board and 4' level to check the floor in the riser area for any dips or rises. If necessary, fill low points or level that part of the floor with a pourable self-leveling product. Measure the space in which the riser will sit to double-check the frame measurements. Cut all the pieces.

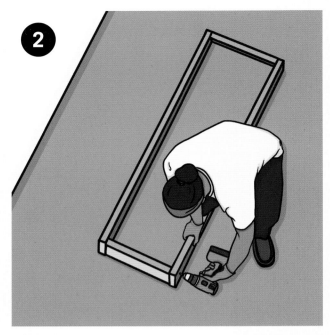

Construct the bottom frame, screwing the ends to the ledgers to create a rectangle. Use a speed square to ensure the inside corners are square, and measure the diagonals after you complete the frame to check square before attaching the frame to the walls.

Secure the frame in position. This may be a tight squeeze, but check the frame for level before screwing it to the wall studs along the back and on the sides. Screw it to the walls using 3" deck screws or masonry fasteners if necessary.

Measure and mark the placement of the bottom frame center joist centered between front and back, and running parallel to them. Screw the joist in place by driving 3" deck screws toe-nail style through the joist and into either end of the frame.

5

Build the top frame as you did the bottom, only with additional pieces to frame out the 12" deep × 18" wide step cut-out, and joists running front to back rather than side to side. Place the top frame on the bottom frame. Check for level and shim as necessary. Toe-screw the frames together.

6

Install insulation hangers across the joists. Fill the joists cavities with rock wool batting. *Note: You can avoid this step and just layer rock wool from the bottom up in each cavity, which will increase the sound-dampening properties of the insulation.*

7

Lay a bead of construction adhesive along the top edge of the frame, including the tops of the joists. Screw the OSB subfloor board to the top of the frame using 2" deck screws.

8

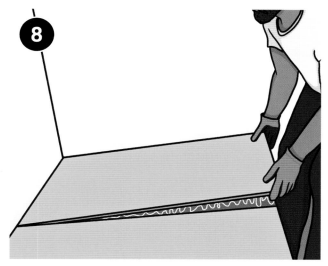

Spread construction adhesive all over the surface and lay a second layer of OSB board, staggering seams so none overlap. Fasten OSB board on top of the step cutout. Finish the riser with carpet as shown here, paint it, or match the flooring you're using in the rest of the room. *NOTE: This may involve fastening decorative 1× fascia boards—finished to match flooring—to the front of the riser.*

How to Wall-Mount a Flat-Panel TV

TOOLS + MATERIALS

Tape measure
Carpenter's pencil
Level
Circular saw or table saw
Drill and bits
Speed square
Mallet
(7) 2 × 6" × 10' pressure treated pine
(4) 4 × 8' OSB subfloor panels

3" deck screws
Construction adhesive
Caulk gun
Rock wool
Insulation hangers (optional)
Straightedge
Serrated knife
Work gloves

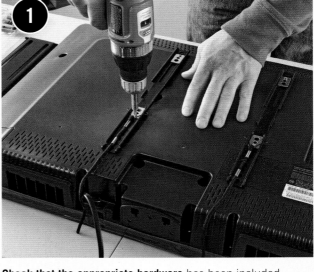

Check that the appropriate hardware has been included with your TV mount. Pry off any plastic caps covering the mounting screw holes in the back of the TV. Lay the TV face down on a soft, cloth-covered surface and screw the mounting bracket to the the back of the TV. Be careful not to overtighten the screws. Remove the TV's base and lay the unit on its back in a safe location.

Locate the studs for the wall mount using a studfinder, and mark the stud centers. If you planning on running in-wall cable to the back of the TV, use your studfinder (if it's capable) to check for any plumbing or electrical in the wall cavity.

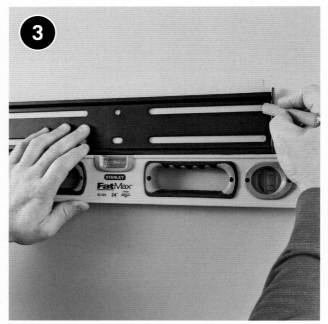

Measure up from the floor and mark for the bottom edge of the wall mount at the stud locations. The center of the TV should be located at the eye level of someone seated across from the TV—usually 40" to 42" from the floor. Use a level to draw a guideline for the bottom of the mount.

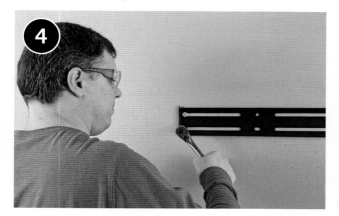

Position the wall-mount plate, check for level with a torpedo level, and mark the screw holes. Drill pilot holes for the mounting screws. Screw the mounting plate into the wall studs, using the supplied fasteners.

Hook up all cables and slide the TV brackets into the wall mount. Although you can buy wall-mount brackets that allow for multi-angle positioning, those won't be necessary in most basements. Look for a basic, non-tilting mounting bracket that is low-profile, sturdy, relatively easy to install, and inexpensive.

ACCOMMODATING MOUNTING VARIATIONS

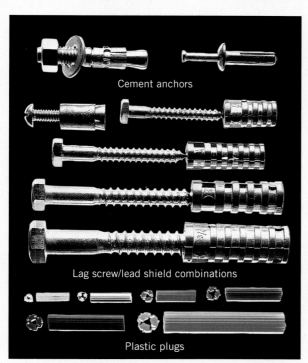

Cement anchors

Lag screw/lead shield combinations

Plastic plugs

In some situations, it just may not be possible to attach a flat-panel TV wall mount to wall studs. In those situations, you'll need to use the appropriate wall anchor. You'll find a large selection of wall anchors at hardware stores and home centers, including specific types meant for plaster, concrete, or brick. Plastic plugs are used for anchoring in hollow walls, while metal work better in masonry and stone. In any case, always use an anchor rated for more than the weight of whatever you intend to hang on the wall.

Given the range of manufacturers, TV technologies, and sizes, mounting your flat-screen TV may be distinctly different from what's shown here. Fixed mounts like the one shown in this project are the simplest and least expensive. However, you can purchase slide bar mounts that are no more complicated to install, but allow minimal adjustment up or down. More versatile extension-arm mounts allow the TV to be pulled away from the wall and angled to either side, to suit the viewers in the room. These usually require additional reinforcement.

Much larger TVs have recently become more widely available and can be the ideal options for luxury basement home theaters. However, mounting any TV 65" or larger means using heavy duty mounts and may entail four-corner support (follow the manufacturer's instructions). In most cases, mounting larger TVs is a job best left to professionals.

Secure Fasteners

The number one concern when mounting any TV should be safety. The second concern should be ensuring no damage is done to what can be incredibly expensive electronics. It's ideal to fasten mounts with lag screws driven into wall studs. Depending on position, that may not be possible. However, given the location, basement theater TVs are just as likely to be mounted to a masonry wall. That's where wall anchors come in. You can select from anchors meant to be driven into drywall, masonry, or even stone. In any case, choose an anchor rated for more than weight of the TV.

How to Install Cable Cover Raceway

Extra wide, paintable plastic raceways conceal the cables and power cords for a wall-mounted TV and can be painted to match the wall after they are installed.

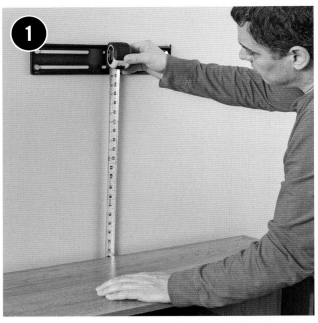

Measure from the components to the wall mount for the TV to determine how long the raceway should be. If you're running the raceway down the wall and then along the length of the wall, subtract the height of a corner piece from the final length of the raceway. Measure and cut each section of raceway separately.

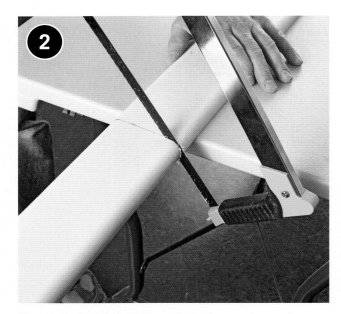

Measure and mark the raceway base piece and cover for cutting. It's a good idea to add 1" to 2" to the length, to ensure that the ends are hidden. Use a hacksaw to cut both the base and the cover.

Use a level to correctly position the base on the wall, and mark the screw holes. Use a studfinder to check stud position. You can drill the base directly into a stud; otherwise, you'll need to screw in drywall anchors, and then screw the base to the anchors.

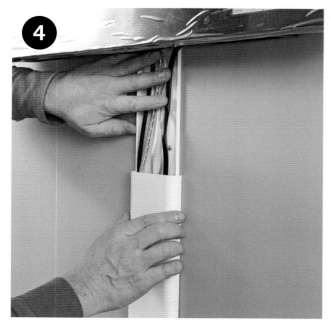

4

Lay the cables down the base, and snap the top half of the cover over the lower half of the base (if your raceway has individual cable channels, align the cables in the channels before installing the cover). Slide the cover up the base until the cables are completely concealed.

5

Paint the cable cover to match the wall. Attach the TV to the wall mount, connect the cables to the TV, and then connect the other ends of the cables to the home theater components.

HOME THEATER SOUND

As incredible as the picture quality of modern flat panel TVs might be, the sound coming out of those TVs is another case entirely. Making TVs thinner has diminished the potential to include quality integral speakers. That's why anyone purchasing a TV would be foolish not to consider adding a soundbar to the system at the very least, and a 5.1 Bluetooth surround-sound speaker system to replicate a truly cinematic experience.

The wireless components available today can make enjoying a luxury sound system as easy as clicking through a few setup screens. Although you can add an amplifier, most speakers and soundbars can be driven right from TV's system settings. Soundbars can be placed on a stand or wall mounted, and the same is true of Bluetooth speakers. Many are completely cordless, and are simply recharged when the battery runs low.

Using these types of speakers allows you to place them exactly where they need to go to create an authentic surround-sound experience, without the hassle of running cables throughout the basement home theater.

Laundry Center

Many of the areas where we do our laundry lack two important features: organization and lighting. This basement or garage laundry center is a self-contained built-in that functions like a room within a room, adding both storage space and task lighting for what can otherwise be a disagreeable task. It is built from a base cabinet and butcher block countertop on one side of a 24-inch-wide, seven-foot-tall stub wall, and a bank of wall cabinets on the other side of the wall. The cabinets are designed to fit above a washer and dryer combo. The structure includes a ceiling with light fixtures mounted over both sides, and a switch wired into the stub wall to control the lights. The walls are built from inexpensive wall sheathing and, along with the ceiling, are clad with easy-to-wash tileboard that adds brightness while contrasting with the maple wood of the cabinets. The edges of the center are trimmed with clear maple.

If you are creating your built-in laundry center in a room that did not previously house your washer and dryer, arrange for and have installed the hookups for both appliances before you build. If you are not experienced with plumbing and wiring, hire a plumber and electrician to run any new drain, supply, dryer vent, or electrical service lines. Also make sure to identify potential sources for electrical service to power the lights (in the version seen here, we installed recessed canister lights over the countertop and above the washer and dryer).

A few well appointed stock cabinets and some modest carpentry skills are the main tools you need to convert basement or garage floor space into an efficient and handsome laundry center.

INSTALL A RECESSED WASHING MACHINE BOX

A recessed washing machine box not only makes your laundry area neater, it reduces the chances of damaging supply connections. If the box includes an opening for the washing machine drain hose, it must be located near a utility sink so you can tie into the sink drain with a standpipe. Normally the hot and cold hose bibs (faucets) in the washing machine box tie into nearby supply tubes for the utility sink. But you can splice into any supply lines that are convenient.

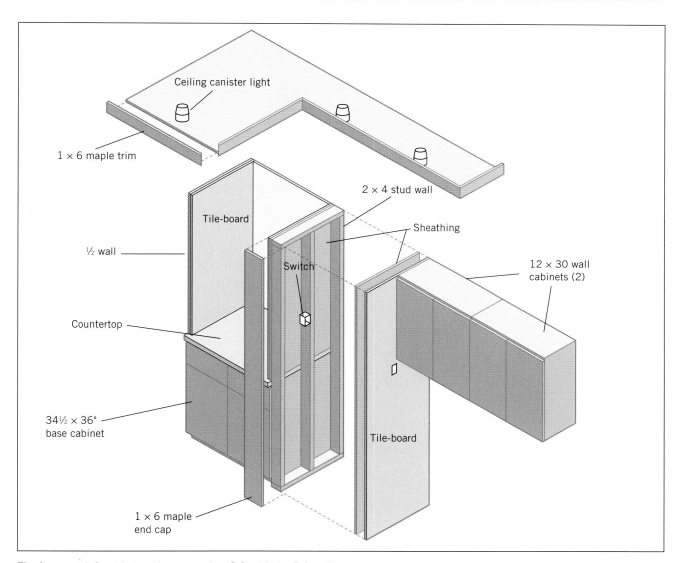

The framework for this laundry center is a 2-ft-wide by 7-ft.-tall stub wall. The folding area is a standard base cabinet with a butcher block countertop, and the center is covered with an L-shaped panel containing task lighting. A bank of wall cabinets fits over the machine locations.

How to Build a Laundry Center

Frame and finish laundry room walls and then attach the sole plate for the partition wall. Locate the wall so the base cabinet (here, 36" wide) will fit between the clad stub wall and the room wall.

Attach the cap plate and studs to finish the stub wall framing. The wall stud that fits against the back wall should fall over a stud location for sturdy fastening. If it does not, you'll need to cut open the wall and install 2 × 4 blocking between the studs to tie into.

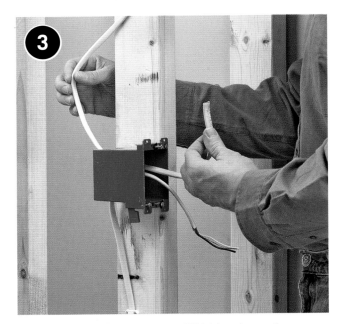

Install a switch box in the wall at 48" high to house the switch for the task lights, if you wish to include them. Run nonmetallic sheathed cable through holes in the studs making sure to staple it within 8" of the box. Run cable to the power source but don't hook it up yet. Run cable from the switch to the junction box or boxes in the task lighting fixtures.

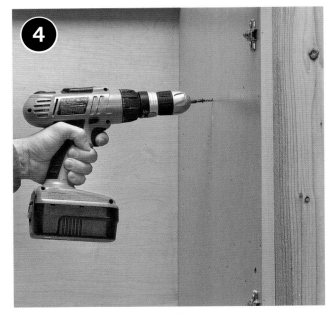

Install a base cabinet (36" wide as shown) between the stub wall and the corner of the room. Anchor the cabinet by driving screws into framing members on each side. For the most pleasing results, choose a base cabinet that matches the wall cabinets you'll be installing over the laundry machines.

Cut a piece of countertop to fit and attach it to the top nailing strips on the base cabinet. Choose a material with a nice smooth surface that is easy to clean. Butcher block is shown here, but a less extravagant material like postform will do.

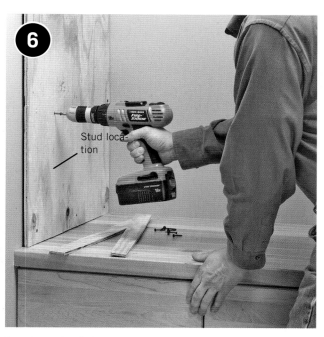

Attach a strip of ½" plywood sheathing to the corner wall to make a spacer/backer for the tileboard surface. Drive wallboard screws at stud locations. Apply a few beads of panel adhesive to the back of the panel first for extra holding power.

Also attach plywood sheathing to the stub wall framing. Make a cutout for the light switch box on the laundry machine side of the stub wall.

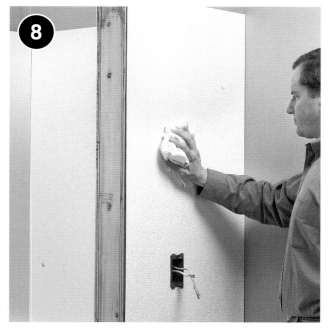

Cut strips of tileboard to fit the wall surfaces, and attach them with panel adhesive. Rub back and forth over the tileboard surface with a clean rag to set the bond. If any tileboard sticks out past the wall edges, trim it off with a utility knife.

(continued)

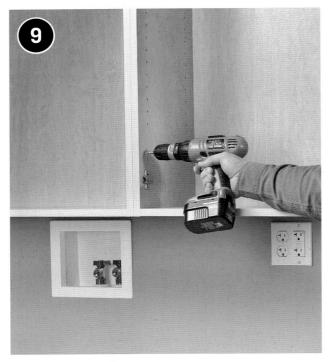

Mount the upper wall cabinets so the cabinet tops are flush with the top of the stub wall. You can tack a temporary ledger to the wall directly below the cabinets to support them while you install fasteners. Drive screws through the nailing strips in the backs of the cabinets at wall stud locations. Then, fasten the cabinets to one another with a few ⅞" screws.

Cut a piece of plywood sheathing so it will fit over the laundry folding area and the wall cabinets—this will have an L shape in most cases. Create enough overhang in front of the wall cabinets that you can mount a small recessed task light if you choose. Glue tileboard to the underside of the ceiling to make a clean, bright surface.

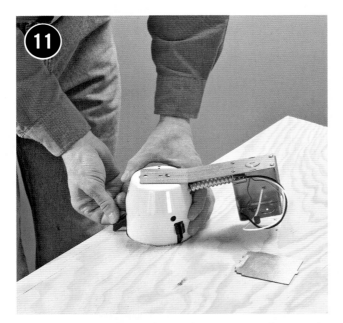

Make cutouts and mount the light fixture to the ceiling panel before you install it. Look for low-profile canister lights to fit the space. Here, one light is positioned over the folding area and two are recessed above the wall cabinets. They are wired together in series.

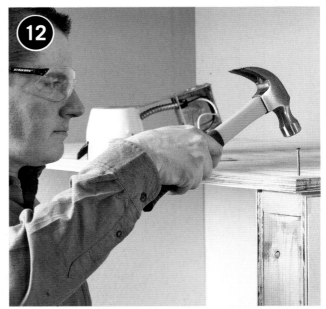

Attach the ceiling panel to the top of the stub wall and to the wall cabinet tops. Also secure it to the top of the backer panel in the corner.

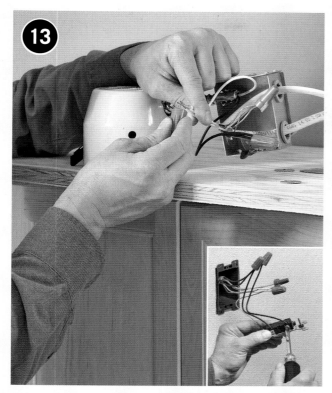

Make the wiring hookups at the light fixtures and at the switch. Shut off power at the main service panel and connect the power lead to your power source. Restore power and test the lights.

Attach strips of 1 × 4 hardwood (maple is seen here) to conceal top gaps and create a visual baffle for the light cans. You can find premilled hardwood at most lumber yards in standard dimensions.

Attach hardwood strips to cover the front of the stub wall. Attach narrower strips to cover the edges of the backer and tileboard in the corner. This strip should run from the countertop to the underside of the ceiling trim strip.

Install your washer and dryer. Front-loading models work best in this situation because they create convenient horizontal surfaces. But top loaders will also fit.

Home Office

Whether it's primarily used for running a business or paying personal bills, a home office is a more productive setting if it's separated from everyday household traffic and noise. In a basement or garage, the wide-open space is ideal for creating a large, formal office, but a quiet corner can be perfect for a small work station. Walkout basements and garages are especially suitable for offices that receive visitors and clients, because they have their own outside entrances. You can add signage or landscape around the entrance to give it a professional appearance. But be sure to check the zoning requirements in your area regarding public office space.

Keep in mind that basement or garage offices need plenty of lighting. An office that's too dark will be unappealing—to you and to clients. If possible, plan your office around an existing window, or add a window for more natural light. If the office has no windows, use abundant ambient lighting to give the room a general sense of warmth.

Planning a basement or garage office that works for you involves many factors, including determining the best layout for your needs, ensuring comfort over long hours of work, and providing the necessary hookups for your equipment.

ELECTRICAL NEEDS

It's a good idea to have access to one or more new circuits that serve only your home office equipment. This will reduce the chances of downtimes caused by circuit overloads. To determine how much power is needed for your equipment, add up the amperage (amps) drawn by all of the pieces. The amps should be listed on the back of each device. The total number of amps used on one circuit should not exceed 80 percent of the circuit's rating. Install enough receptacles to accommodate the devices you currently have, as well as a few extras for equipment you may need in the future.

Also make sure you have all the communications wiring you'll need—for internet access, fax machines, business and personal phone lines, etc. As with the electrical outlets, including extra wiring and jacks now may be far more convenient and cost-effective than adding them later.

A home office needn't be elaborate. If it's thoughtfully designed, even the smallest area can be an efficient workspace. Nor does a home office necessarily need its own room. In shared spaces, however, everyone will feel more comfortable if there is some sense of division or an implied boundary, such as a standing screen, curtain, bookcase, or lowered ceiling.

BOOSTING SIGNALS

Basements can be dead zones for wireless signals. This can spell big trouble in the modern home office. Make sure your internet connection is as strong as necessary, by using a wifi range extender—essentially a second wireless router—or software to increase the range of your existing router.

If you're having problems getting a signal on your cell phone and you don't have a landline, you might consider adding a repeater system. This involves using an outdoor antenna routed to a broadcaster inside. It can effectively boost the signal so that you don't have to fight to get bars on your phone.

These typical office layouts can help you find a configuration that will work for your given space. To help with your planning, think about the tasks you do most often and how much storage space you'll need for commonly used materials. Approximate sizes are given for each typical office element.

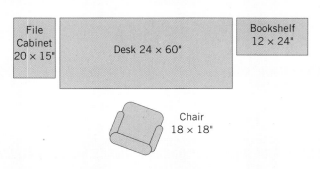

Wall Layout. With this simple layout, the desk and storage units are aligned along one wall. Although this is a good choice for offices with limited space, it is less efficient than other arrangements because the elements are not always within easy reach.

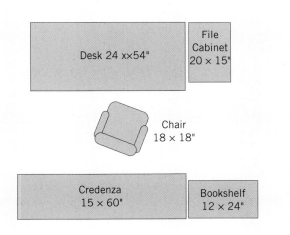

Parallel Layout. In this arrangement, there are two desks or tables set a few feet apart from each other with a chair in between. A parallel layout makes it easy to separate your work by task; for example, you can set your computer on one surface and place your files and phone on the other.

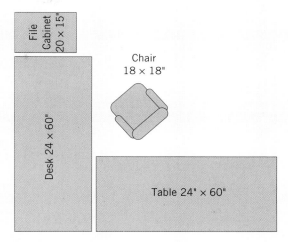

L-shaped Layout. This configuration is the most effective for a corner. You can also use it to divide a space, by placing one leg of the L against a wall and letting the other leg project out into the room. The L shape gives you fairly easy access to a large work surface.

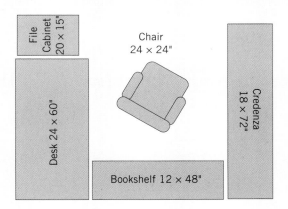

U-shaped Layout. This layout creates the most efficient work area because all of the elements are within easy reach. By adding a chair on the outside of one of the work surfaces, you can create a small conference area. But this is also the most space-consuming layout, and depending on your garage or basement, you may not have the floor space to create this layout with enough area around it for free movement.

Conversion Charts

ENGLISH TO METRIC

TO CONVERT:	TO:	MULTIPLY BY:
Inches	Millimeters	25.4
Inches	Centimeters	2.54
Feet	Meters	0.305
Yards	Meters	0.914
Square inches	Square centimeters	6.45
Square feet	Square meters	0.093
Square yards	Square meters	0.836
Ounces	Milliliters	30.0
Pints (US)	Liters	0.473 (Imp. 0.568)
Quarts (US)	Liters	0.946 (Imp. 1.136)
Gallons (US)	Liters	3.785 (Imp. 4.546)
Ounces	Grams	28.4
Pounds	Kilograms	0.454

TO CONVERT:	TO:	MULTIPLY BY:
Millimeters	Inches	0.039
Centimeters	Inches	0.394
Meters	Feet	3.28
Meters	Yards	1.09
Square centimeters	Square inches	0.155
Square meters	Square feet	10.8
Square meters	Square yards	1.2
Milliliters	Ounces	.033
Liters	Pints (US)	2.114 (Imp. 1.76)
Liters	Quarts (US)	1.057 (Imp. 0.88)
Liters	Gallons (US)	0.264 (Imp. 0.22)
Grams	Ounces	0.035
Kilograms	Pounds	2.2

CONVERTING TEMPERATURES

Convert degrees Fahrenheit (F) to degrees Celsius (C) by following this simple formula: Subtract 32 from the Fahrenheit temperature reading. Then multiply that number by $\frac{5}{9}$. For example, $77°F - 32 = 45$. $45 \times \frac{5}{9} = 25°C$.

To convert degrees Celsius to degrees Fahrenheit, multiply the Celsius temperature reading by $\frac{9}{5}$. Then, add 32. For example, $25°C \times \frac{9}{5} = 45$. $45 + 32 = 77°F$.

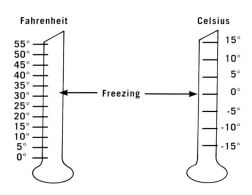

METRIC PLYWOOD PANELS

Metric plywood panels are commonly available in two sizes: 1,200 mm × 2,400 mm and 1,220 mm × 2,400 mm, which is roughly equivalent to a 4 × 8' sheet. Standard and Select sheathing panels come in standard thicknesses, while Sanded grade panels are available in special thicknesses.

STANDARD SHEATHING GRADE		SANDED GRADE	
7.5 mm	(⁵⁄₁₆")	6 mm	(⁴⁄₁₇")
9.5 mm	(³⁄₈")	8 mm	(⁵⁄₁₆")
12.5 mm	(½")	11 mm	(⁷⁄₁₆")
15.5 mm	(⁵⁄₈")	14 mm	(⁹⁄₁₆")
18.5 mm	(¾")	17 mm	(²⁄₃")
20.5 mm	(¹³⁄₁₆")	19 mm	(¾")
22.5 mm	(⅞")	21 mm	(¹³⁄₁₆")
25.5 mm	(1")	24 mm	(¹⁵⁄₁₆")

LUMBER DIMENSIONS

NOMINAL - U.S.	ACTUAL - U.S. (IN INCHES)	METRIC
1 × 2	¾ × 1½	19 × 38 mm
1 × 3	¾ × 2½	19 × 64 mm
1 × 4	¾ × 3½	19 × 89 mm
1 × 5	¾ × 4½	19 × 114 mm
1 × 6	¾ × 5½	19 × 140 mm
1 × 7	¾ × 6¼	19 × 159 mm
1 × 8	¾ × 7¼	19 × 184 mm
1 × 10	¾ × 9¼	19 × 235 mm
1 × 12	¾ × 11¼	19 × 286 mm
1¼ × 4	1 × 3½	25 × 89 mm
1¼ × 6	1 × 5½	25 × 140 mm
1¼ × 8	1 × 7¼	25 × 184 mm
1¼ × 10	1 × 9¼	25 × 235 mm
1¼ × 12	1 × 11¼	25 × 286 mm
1½ × 4	1¼ × 3½	32 × 89 mm
1½ × 6	1¼ × 5½	32 × 140 mm
1½ × 8	1¼ × 7¼	32 × 184 mm
1½ × 10	1¼ × 9¼	32 × 235 mm
1½ × 12	1¼ × 11¼	32 × 286 mm
2 × 4	1½ × 3½	38 × 89 mm
2 × 6	1½ × 5½	38 × 140 mm
2 × 8	1½ × 7¼	38 × 184 mm
2 × 10	1½ × 9¼	38 × 235 mm
2 × 12	1½ × 11¼	38 × 286 mm
3 × 6	2½ × 5½	64 × 140 mm
4 × 4	3½ × 3½	89 × 89 mm
4 × 6	3½ × 5½	89 × 140 mm

LIQUID MEASUREMENT EQUIVALENTS

1 Pint	= 16 Fluid Ounces	= 2 Cups
1 Quart	= 32 Fluid Ounces	= 2 Pints
1 Gallon	= 128 Fluid Ounces	= 4 Quarts

DRILL BIT GUIDE

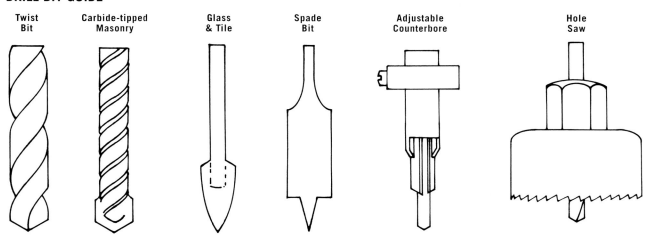

Twist Bit · Carbide-tipped Masonry · Glass & Tile · Spade Bit · Adjustable Counterbore · Hole Saw

NAILS

Nail lengths are identified by numbers from 4 to 60 followed by the letter "d," which stands for "penny." For general framing and repair work, use common or box nails. Common nails are best suited to framing work where strength is important. Box nails are smaller in diameter than common nails, which makes them easier to drive and less likely to split wood. Use box nails for light work and thin materials. Most common and box nails have a cement or vinyl coating that improves their holding power.

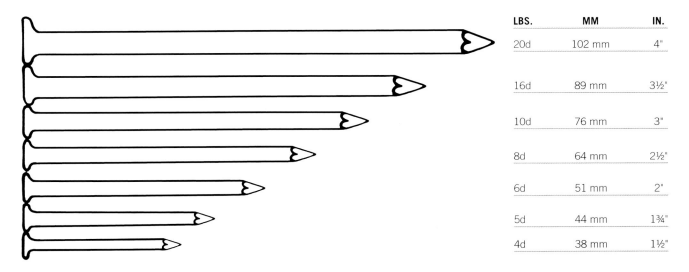

LBS.	MM	IN.
20d	102 mm	4"
16d	89 mm	3½"
10d	76 mm	3"
8d	64 mm	2½"
6d	51 mm	2"
5d	44 mm	1¾"
4d	38 mm	1½"

COUNTERBORE, SHANK + PILOT HOLE DIAMETERS

SCREW SIZE	COUNTERBORE DIAMETER FOR SCREW HEAD (IN INCHES)	CLEARANCE HOLE FOR SCREW SHANK (IN INCHES)	PILOT HOLE DIAMETER	
			HARD WOOD (IN INCHES)	SOFT WOOD (IN INCHES)
#1	.146 (9/64)	5/64	3/64	1/32
#2	¼	3/32	3/64	1/32
#3	¼	7/64	1/16	3/64
#4	¼	⅛	1/16	3/64
#5	¼	⅛	5/64	1/16
#6	5/16	9/64	3/32	5/64
#7	5/16	5/32	3/32	5/64
#8	⅜	11/64	⅛	3/32
#9	⅜	11/64	⅛	3/32
#10	⅜	3/16	⅛	7/64
#11	½	3/16	5/32	9/64
#12	½	7/32	9/64	⅛

Resources

Acoustic Frontiers, LLC
415-524-8741
acousticfrontiers.com

American Institute of Architects
(800) 242 3837
www.aia.org

American Society of Interior Designers
202-546-3480
www.asid.org

Armstrong World Industries
Flooring and ceiling tiles
717-397-0611
www.armstrongceilings.com

Association of Home Appliance Manufacturers
202-872-5955
www.aham.org

The Capable Group
905-889-0025
capablegroupinc.ca

Fusion Bowling
Bowling lanes featured on page 10.
904-701-2695
hello@fusionbowling.com
www.fusionbowling.com

International Code Council
888-ICC-SAFE (888-422-7233), option 0
www.iccsafe.org

National Association of the Remodeling Industry
1-847-298-9200
www.nari.org

National Kitchen & Bath Association (NKBA)
800-843-6522
www.nkba.com

U.S. Environmental Protection Agency Indoor air quality
www.epa.gov/indoor-air-quality-iaq

Window Well Experts
Basement window well access as shown on page 187.
888-650-9355
info@windowwellexperts.com
windowwellexperts.com

Photo Credits

p. 6 Elizabeth Whiting & Associates / www.ewastock.com

p. 16 © Anne Gummerson / www.AnneGummersonPhoto.com

p. 8 (top) © Beth Singer / www.BethSingerPhotographer.com

p. 8 (bottom) © Jeff Kruegar for Crystal Cabinets

p. 9 (both) Courtesy of the Capable Group

p. 10 (top) Courtesy of Fusion Bowling

p. 10 (bottom) Courtesy of the Capable Group

p. 11 Courtesy of the Capable Group

p. 12 (both) Courtesy of the Capable Group

p. 13 (top) Beth Singer

p. 13 (bottom) California Closets

p. 18 Courtesy of the Capable Group

p. 40 (lower left) Courtesy of Dow AgroSciences LLC (Sentricon Termite Colony Elimination System)

p. 48 Shutterstock/Charise Wilson

p. 57 (top right) Courtesy of the National Fire Protection Association (NFPA), www.nfpa.org

p. 66 California Closets

p. 74 Shutterstock

p. 79 Shutterstock/Sheila Say

p. 92 photo courtesy of Room & Board® / www.RoomAndBoard.com

p. 112 Courtesy of the Capable Group

p. 154 Shutterstock/Hendrickson Photography

p. 162 Shutterstock/pics721

p. 163 Shutterstock/be intrigued

p. 182 Courtesy of the Capable Group

p. 184 Courtesy of the Capable Group

p. 186 Photos courtesy of Moen, www.moen.com, (800) 289-6636

p. 187 (left) Courtesy Window Well Experts

p. 202 Shutterstock / © Pablo Scapinachis

p. 216 Courtesy of Acoustic Frontiers, LLC

p. 218 Shutterstock/pics721

p. 225 Shutterstock/asiandelight

Index